FIRST FLOOR

S E ○ W N

INDEPENDENCE AVENUE ENTRANCE

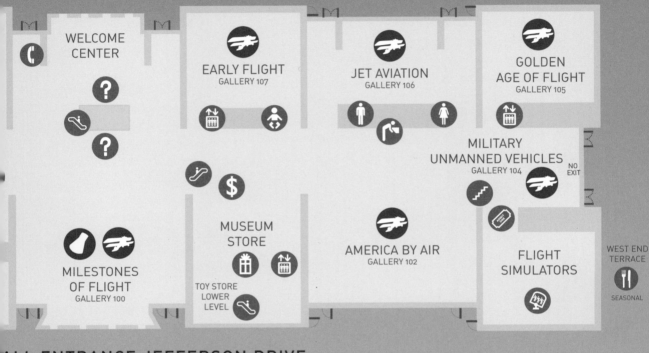

WELCOME CENTER

EARLY FLIGHT
GALLERY 107

JET AVIATION
GALLERY 106

GOLDEN AGE OF FLIGHT
GALLERY 105

MILITARY UNMANNED VEHICLES
GALLERY 104

NO EXIT

MILESTONES OF FLIGHT
GALLERY 100

MUSEUM STORE

TOY STORE LOWER LEVEL

AMERICA BY AIR
GALLERY 102

FLIGHT SIMULATORS

WEST END TERRACE

SEASONAL

MALL ENTRANCE JEFFERSON DRIVE

 Baby Care Station

 Men's Restroom

 Women's Restroom

 Family Restroom

 Water Fountain

 Food Service

 Simulators

 Tickets

 Theater

 Telephones

 Elevator

 Escalator

 Stairs

 ATM

OFFICIAL GUIDE TO THE SMITHSONIAN

NATIONAL AIR AND SPACE MUSEUM

THIRD EDITION

BELL X-1 * APOLLO 11 * SPIRIT OF ST. LOUIS * SPACESHIPONE * X-15 * VIKING LANDER * BELL XP-59A AIRACOMET * BOEING 747 * CURTISS JN-4D JENNY * DOUGLAS DC-3 * AIRBUS A320 * HUGHES H-1 * FRIENDSHIP 7 * X-15 * FORD 5-AT TRI-MOTOR * DOUGLAS DC-3 * BOEING 747 * PREDATOR * HUGHES H-1 * BEECH STAGGERWING * WITTMAN BUSTER * POLAR STAR * CURTISS ROBIN "OLE MISS" * MESSERSCHMITT ME 262 * LOCKHEED XP-80 * FH-1 PHANTOM * LILIENTHAL GLIDER * WRIGHT MILITARY FLYER * CURTISS MODEL D "HEADLESS PUSHER" * CURTISS MOTORCYCLE * ECKER FLYING BOAT * BLÉRIOT XI * BOEING 757 FUSELAGE * CESSNA 150 * DE HAVILLAND DH-4 * LOCKHEED U-2 * TIROS I * GOES SATELLITE * EARLY INSTRUMENTS * MOUNT WILSON OBSERVING CAGE * HUBBLE SPACE TELESCOPE MIRROR * LUNAR MODULE * LUNAR SPACECRAFT * V-2 MISSILE * APOLLO-SOYUZ TEST PROJECT * M2-F3 LIFTING BODY * SKYLAB * CONCORDE * ENOLA GAY * LOCKHEED SR-71 BLACKBIRD * DOUGLAS SBD DAUNTLESS * SPACE HANGAR * GRUMMAN WILDCAT * DOUGLAS A-4C SKYHAWK * BOEING F4B-4 * SUPERMARINE SPITFIRE * NORTH AMERICAN P-51 MUSTANG * MACCHI FOLGORE * MITSUBISHI ZERO * MESSERSCHMITT BF 109 * FOKKER D.VII * SPAD XIII * VOISIN VIII * ALBATROS D.VA * VOYAGER * MARS EXPLORATION ROVER * FOKKER T-2 * LOCKHEED 5B VEGA * WRIGHT EX "VIN FIZ" * DOUGLAS WORLD CRUISER * CURTISS R3C * LOCKHEED 8 SIRIUS * EXPLORER II * WRIGHT BICYCLE * GRUMMAN X-29 * HIMAT * IRIDIUM SATELLITE * BELL X-1 * APOLLO 11 * SPIRIT OF ST. LOUIS * SPACESHIPONE * X-15 * VIKING LANDER * BELL XP-59A AIRACOMET * BOEING 747 * CURTISS JN-4D JENNY * DOUGLAS DC-3 * AIRBUS A320 * HUGHES H-1 * FRIENDSHIP 7 * X-15 * FORD 5-AT TRI-MOTOR * DOUGLAS DC-3 * BOEING 747 * PREDATOR * HUGHES H-1 * BEECH STAGGERWING * WITTMAN BUSTER * POLAR STAR * CURTISS ROBIN "OLE MISS" * MESSERSCHMITT ME 262 * LOCKHEED XP-80 * FH-1 PHANTOM * LILIENTHAL GLIDER * WRIGHT MILITARY FLYER * CURTISS MODEL D "HEADLESS PUSHER" * CURTISS MOTORCYCLE * ECKER FLYING BOAT * BLÉRIOT XI * BOEING 757 FUSELAGE * CESSNA 150 * DE HAVILLAND DH-4 * LOCKHEED U-2 * TIROS I * GOES SATELLITE * EARLY INSTRUMENTS * MOUNT WILSON OBSERVING CAGE * HUBBLE SPACE TELESCOPE MIRROR * LUNAR MODULE * LUNAR SPACECRAFT * V-2 MISSILE * APOLLO-SOYUZ TEST PROJECT * M2-F3 LIFTING BODY * SKYLAB * CONCORDE * ENOLA GAY * LOCKHEED SR-71 BLACKBIRD * DOUGLAS SBD DAUNTLESS * SPACE HANGAR * GRUMMAN WILDCAT * DOUGLAS A-4C SKYHAWK * BOEING F4B-4 * SUPERMARINE SPITFIRE * NORTH AMERICAN P-51 MUSTANG * MACCHI FOLGORE * MITSUBISHI ZERO * MESSERSCHMITT BF 109 * FOKKER D.VII * SPAD XIII * VOISIN VIII * ALBATROS D.VA * VOYAGER * MARS EXPLORATION ROVER * FOKKER T-2 * LOCKHEED 5B VEGA * WRIGHT EX "VIN FIZ" * DOUGLAS WORLD CRUISER * CURTISS R3C * LOCKHEED 8 SIRIUS * EXPLORER II * WRIGHT BICYCLE * GRUMMAN X-29 * HIMAT * IRIDIUM SATELLITE * BELL X-1 * APOLLO 11 * SPIRIT OF ST. LOUIS * SPACESHIPONE * X-15 * VIKING LANDER * BELL XP-59A AIRACOMET * BOEING 747 * CURTISS JN-4D JENNY * DOUGLAS DC-3 * AIRBUS A320 * HUGHES H-1 * FRIENDSHIP 7 * X-15 * FORD 5-AT TRI-MOTOR * DOUGLAS DC-3 * BOEING 747 * PREDATOR * HUGHES H-1 * BEECH STAGGERWING * WITTMAN BUSTER * POLAR STAR * CURTISS ROBIN "OLE MISS" * MESSERSCHMITT ME 262 * LOCKHEED XP-80 * FH-1 PHANTOM * LILIENTHAL GLIDER * WRIGHT MILITARY FLYER * CURTISS MODEL D "HEADLESS PUSHER" * CURTISS MOTORCYCLE * ECKER FLYING BOAT * BLÉRIOT XI * BOEING 757 FUSELAGE * CESSNA 150 * DE HAVILLAND DH-4 * LOCKHEED U-2 * TIROS I * GOES SATELLITE * EARLY INSTRUMENTS * MOUNT WILSON OBSERVING CAGE * HUBBLE SPACE TELESCOPE MIRROR * LUNAR MODULE * LUNAR SPACECRAFT * V-2 MISSILE * ENOLA GAY

OFFICIAL GUIDE TO THE SMITHSONIAN

NATIONAL AIR AND SPACE MUSEUM

THIRD EDITION

SMITHSONIAN BOOKS
WASHINGTON, DC

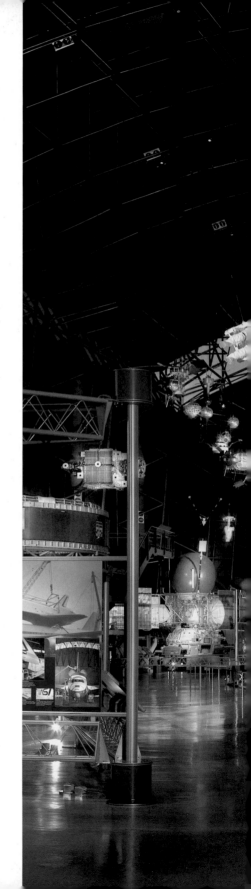

Official Guide to the National Air and Space Museum, Third Edition

Library of Congress Cataloging-in-Publication Data
National Air and Space Museum.
Official guide to the National Air and Space Museum. – 3rd ed.
    p. cm.
    ISBN 978-1-58834-267-6
  1. National Air and Space Museum–Guidebooks. 2. Aeronautical museums–Washington
    (D.C.)–Guidebooks. 3. Astronautical museums–Washington (D.C.)–Guidebooks.
    4.Washington (D.C.)–Guidebooks. I. Title.
    TL506.U6W376 2009
    629.130074'753–dc22   2009026695

Guidebook Staff
National Air and Space Museum
Writer: David A. Romanowski, Exhibits Design Division

Smithsonian Books
Editor: Christina Wiginton
Copy Editor: Lise Sajewski
Production Assistants: Michelle Lecuyer, Kathryn Murphy
Design: Jody Billert / Design Literate, Inc.

Acknowledgments
We would like to thank those at the National Air and Space Museum who reviewed parts
of the manuscript, assisted in photo research, provided images, or offered support for
this new edition: Barbara Brennan, Jon Hallenberg, Kathleen Hanser, Peter Jakab, Brian
Mullen, Jennifer O'Brien, and Dane Penland. Special thanks to Eric Long for taking
many new photographs for this edition.

Right: Surrounded by exhibit cases,
rockets, missiles, satellites, and
other artifacts, the Space Shuttle
Enterprise is the centerpiece of the
Space Hangar.

Half Title Page: A section of a
study for one of two murals that
cover the walls of the Museum's
South Lobby and extend upward
to the second-floor ceiling. Robert
T. McCall's *The Space Mural: A
Cosmic View*, was created for the
National Air and Space Museum's
opening in 1976; these murals
symbolize the Museum's dual
themes of air and space.

TABLE OF

CONTENTS

 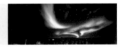

Welcome *to the* Museum

John R. Dailey, director of the National Air and Space Museum.

Opposite: The National Air and Space Museum with the U.S. Capitol in the background.

Welcome to the Smithsonian's National Air and Space Museum. Since it opened on the National Mall in Washington, D.C., on July 1, 1976, the Museum has welcomed over a quarter billion visitors from across the nation and around the world. Americans are justly proud of this institution, and those of us working here are tremendously proud to be a part of it.

Our official purpose, to paraphrase the law that established the Museum, is to memorialize the national development of aviation and spaceflight by collecting, preserving, and displaying historical artifacts, engaging in historical and scientific research, and providing educational opportunities for the public. I like to boil down our mission to three simple words: commemorate, educate, and inspire.

The word "inspire" doesn't appear in our founding legislation, but it underlies everything we are about. The National Air and Space Museum is more than just a place to examine our past and celebrate yesterday's technological achievements; it is also about looking toward the future and exciting new generations of doers and seekers and dreamers. The sparkle in a child's eye when he or she sees the 1903 Wright Flyer for the first time, or looks into the Apollo 11 command module, or touches a piece of the Moon—that's one important measure of our success.

We carry out our mission in many ways, some quite obvious to our visitors, others not. We are famous, of course, for our unparalleled collections and displays of historical aircraft and spacecraft, but there is much more that goes on here: tours and educational programs; lectures, films, and planetarium shows; historical and scientific research; the collection and care of artifacts and archival materials; public service and outreach; events and celebrations. This guide focuses not only on what you will see in our exhibition galleries when you visit, but also upon these other aspects.

We are a constantly growing and evolving institution. On December 15, 2003, we opened a new facility to house most of the collections once stored at our venerable Paul E. Garber Facility. The Steven F. Udvar-Hazy Center near Washington Dulles International Airport in Northern Virginia is a spectacular, state-of-the-art addition to the National Air and Space Museum. Here you can view even more aircraft, spacecraft, and other artifacts than we can display at our museum on the National Mall. This guide provides a preview of what you will find there.

So sit back and enjoy this armchair tour through the world's most popular museum. I hope it inspires you to visit us again soon.

J. R. DAILEY
DIRECTOR
NATIONAL AIR AND SPACE MUSEUM

Staff, volunteers, and docents at the Museum's Welcome Center greet visitors and provide information, directions, and advice.

Opposite: Visitors in the *Milestones of Flight* gallery.

National Air *and* Space Museum

PAST, PRESENT, AND FUTURE

On the morning of July 1, 1976, one of two Viking spacecraft heading toward the first successful landing on Mars sent a signal homeward. Traveling at the speed of light, the signal reached Earth about 18 minutes later and was relayed to the site of a dedication ceremony on the National Mall in Washington, D.C. The signal activated a robotic arm—identical to the arm on the spacecraft itself—that cut a ribbon stretched across the entrance to the Smithsonian's National Air and Space Museum. America's Bicentennial gift to itself was officially open.

The Smithsonian Institution anticipated that its newest museum would receive about three million visitors a year. Twenty-five days after it opened, the Museum welcomed its one-millionth visitor. Twenty-five days after that, it welcomed its two-millionth visitor. Within a year the Museum was the biggest tourist attraction in Washington and on its way to becoming the most visited museum in the world.

It isn't hard to see why. Within its walls of Tennessee pink cedar marble, inside soaring galleries enclosed by sweeping expanses of glass, resides the world's greatest collection of historic aircraft and spacecraft, along with countless other objects memorializing aviation and spaceflight. As overwhelming as this technological treasure trove is, the Museum you experience as a visitor is merely the proverbial tip of a very large iceberg. The National Air and Space Museum is a dynamic, multifaceted institution with an intriguing past and an exciting future.

From "Tin Shed" to Marvel on the Mall

The Museum's incomparable collection began with 20 beautiful Chinese kites given to the Smithsonian by the Chinese Imperial Commission in the late 1800s. The kites had been displayed at the Philadelphia Centennial Exposition of 1876, an event that provided such a bounty of new acquisitions—enough to fill more than 60 railroad boxcars—that the Smithsonian had to build a whole new building next to the Smithsonian Castle to exhibit them. The new National Museum, later renamed the Arts and Industries Building (A&I), opened in 1881. It would eventually serve as home for many of the Smithsonian's prize aircraft and spacecraft.

The Smithsonian had lent its support to aerial activity even before the Civil War, but in 1887 with the appointment of its third secretary, Samuel P. Langley, the Institution became directly involved in the emerging field of aeronautics. Like the Wright brothers, Secretary Langley was determined to create a manned, powered flying machine. He designed and flew a succession of unmanned "aerodromes" before twice trying to launch a manned aircraft—the second attempt took place only nine days before the Wright brothers' historic flights. Both of Langley's attempts failed miserably.

Langley's "Great Aerodrome" did eventually fly—years later and after much modification. The Smithsonian then restored the aircraft to its original condition, put it on display in the Arts and Industries Building, and credited it as the "first man-carrying aeroplane in the history of the world capable of sustained free flight." This misleading claim irked Orville Wright, who ended up sending the 1903 Wright Flyer to the Science Museum in London rather than give it to the Smithsonian. Amends were ultimately made, and the airplane was donated to the Smithsonian upon Orville's death in 1948.

By the early 1900s, the Smithsonian's aircraft collection was small but growing and included Langley's aerodromes and the Wright Military Flyer, the world's first military airplane. As World War I ended, the Smithsonian began to collect examples of other significant military

Opposite: Prompted by a command sent by a Viking spacecraft, a robotic arm cut the ribbon to open the National Air and Space Museum on July 1, 1976. President Gerald Ford, Museum Director and Apollo 11 astronaut Michael Collins, and Smithsonian Secretary S. Dillon Ripley (foreground, left to right) presided over the dedication ceremony.

aircraft. To exhibit them, the Institution took over from the War Department a long metal building standing along Independence Avenue behind the Smithsonian Castle. The new air museum opened to the public in 1920. While considered temporary, the "Tin Shed" would remain in use for the next 55 years.

Also in that banner year of 1920, the Smithsonian made what would prove to be one of its most important acquisitions. His name was Paul E. Garber, a talented young craftsman and model maker who was smitten with the new world of aviation. He began working at the Smithsonian as a preparator, a maker and fixer of exhibits, but he was soon talking people into donating their airplanes—often very historic airplanes—to the Institution. He encouraged the Navy to preserve and part with the NC-4, the first airplane to cross the Atlantic. He then talked a dubious Acting Secretary Charles Abbot into sending a telegram to Charles Lindbergh in Paris, asking him to donate the **Spirit of St. Louis.** A year later Lindbergh delivered the **Spirit** to the Smithsonian, and the airplane was hung in a place of honor in the Arts and Industries Building. Although aviation was generally a low priority at the Smithsonian, over the next few decades Garber managed to build the finest collection of aircraft in the world. They ended up in the Tin Shed, in the A&I Building, or, as in the case of the big NC-4, on loan to other museums.

At the end of World War II, the U.S. Army Air Forces set aside for

The "Tin Shed," a temporary World War I–era metal building behind the Smithsonian Castle, housed many of the Museum's aeronautical artifacts from 1920 to 1975.

Opposite: Gemini IV in *Milestones of Flight.*

preservation a huge collection of Allied and captured Axis aircraft to memorialize its contribution to winning the war. About half of the collection eventually went to the U.S. Air Force Museum near Dayton, Ohio. The rest—an unprecedented bonanza of 97 aircraft and more than 1,300 related objects—was transferred to the Smithsonian by Gen. Henry H. "Hap" Arnold, commander of the U.S. Army Air Forces. General Arnold arranged for their storage at a government-owned aircraft factory on the present-day site of Chicago's O'Hare International Airport, until a suitable place to exhibit them could be found. The U.S. Navy, prompted by a certain Naval Reserve officer named Lt. Paul Garber, had set aside for the Smithsonian representative examples of its own aircraft at Norfolk, Virginia.

General Arnold also worked with Rep. Jennings Randolph of West Virginia, a congressional champion of aviation, to pass legislation creating a separate museum of flight within the Smithsonian. On August 12, 1946, President Harry S. Truman signed the law creating the National Air Museum, which was directed to

> memorialize the national development of aviation; collect, preserve, and display aeronautical equipment of historical significance; serve as a repository for scientific equipment and data pertaining to the development of aviation; and provide educational material for the historical study of aviation.

No funds, however, were set aside to construct a new museum. The Tin Shed and the A&I Building would serve as the National Air Museum for nearly three more decades.

The onset of the Korean War created a storage crisis. The Air Force wanted to reactivate the aircraft factory where Hap Arnold's collection was stored. All those World War II aircraft had to go or face destruction. Paul Garber, back with the Smithsonian after five years in the Navy and now the curator of the National Air Museum, searched the Washington area for a place to relocate the endangered collection. He settled for 21 acres of federally owned woodland at Silver Hill, Maryland, a few miles from the National Mall. Garber acquired the land, talked various military and civilian organizations into donating their resources to clear the site and erect some storage buildings, and eventually got the aircraft and other objects transferred to Silver Hill. Conditions there were far from optimal—many aircraft remained parked outside or packed away in pieces—but Garber had managed to save the collection.

Progress on creating a new museum was slow. Design proposals were developed, and a site was chosen just across Independence Avenue from the Castle, but then that location was lost to another development project. In 1958 Congress and President Dwight D. Eisenhower finally authorized construction on a three-block site on the National Mall; funding, however, remained elusive.

The National Museum of History and Technology (now the National Museum of American History) opened in 1964, and the National Air Museum took over most of the exhibit space in the A&I Building. With the advent of the space age, spacecraft began to take their place beside aircraft, and a row of rockets sprouted outside the west entrance to A&I. In 1966 President Lyndon B. Johnson signed a law amending the National Air Museum's charter legislation to encompass spaceflight. The National Air and Space Museum was born— at least on paper.

It took another six years, public outcry over the deteriorating collections at Silver Hill, and the influential support in Congress of Arizona Sen. Barry Goldwater before $40 million in construction funds was finally appropriated. The museum design proposal was scaled back to fit the budget, and ground was officially broken on November 20, 1972. The monumental task of creating a new national museum began.

Besides the actual building, exhibitions for 23 galleries had to be planned and created. Several major exhibitions were built in advance and opened to the public in the A&I Building. The new museum building was ready for occupancy in 1975, and staff began relocating the aircraft, spacecraft, and exhibits in the Tin Shed and A&I, along

"Rocket Row" in front of the west entrance to the Arts and Industries Building on the National Mall in the 1960s.

with dozens of aircraft restored at Silver Hill. Installation took a year, with the entire staff pitching in to help with final preparations. Three days before the nation's 200th birthday, the Smithsonian's National Air and Space Museum opened to worldwide acclaim.

A Museum for the Second Century of Flight

Since the days of the Tin Shed, the Museum's display and storage space never quite kept up with the growth of its collections. Even the opening of the National Air and Space Museum—filled to rafters as it is with airplanes, spacecraft, and rockets—did not solve the storage problems. Airplanes in particular take up a lot of space. At any given time the Museum displays only about 60 to 65 aircraft—a small fraction of its collection.

If the aircraft, spacecraft, and other artifacts in the collection are to survive indefinitely, as the Museum intends, they require a healthy environment in terms of temperature and humidity. The Paul E. Garber Preservation, Restoration, and Storage Facility at Silver Hill has served nobly since the mid-1950s, but it has never adequately filled

The 1903 Wright Flyer hangs in the main entrance hall to the Smithsonian's Arts and Industries Building in 1973. Behind it is the *Spirit of St. Louis;* above it, the 1909 Wright Military Flyer. On the floor to the right are the Apollo 11 command module *Columbia* and a lunar module. To the left is Gemini IV.

the Museum's preservation and storage needs. And because of the facility's limited public access, most people never got to see the treasures housed there. But all that has changed.

Two days before the 100th anniversary of the Wright brothers' historic 1903 flights, the Museum greeted the second century of flight by opening a spectacular new companion museum. Located on the grounds of Washington Dulles International Airport in Northern Virginia, the Steven F. Udvar-Hazy Center dwarfs in size the Museum on the Mall. It displays over 150 aircraft in its huge Boeing Aviation Hangar and about as many rockets, missiles, satellites, and other spacecraft in its James S. McDonnell Space Hangar, with more artifacts being moved there from the Garber Facility all the time. The Center will eventually house a new and larger restoration facility, an archives, collections processing unit, conservation laboratory, and collections storage for small objects. And best of all, like the Museum on the National Mall, the Udvar-Hazy Center is open to visitors daily, with no reservations or guided tours required.

The Museum Today

As you wander through the exhibit halls, clues to the inner workings of the Museum are all around you. A docent is gathering visitors in *Milestones of Flight* for a free tour. A family is following a self-guided walking-tour brochure. A curator is about to give an informal talk on an airplane in the *World War II Aviation* gallery. A distinguished former astronaut is scheduled to present a lecture that evening in the Museum's theater. In the *How Things Fly* gallery, a student explainer is demonstrating the forces of flight. In the Museum Store, someone is buying one of the dozens of books written or edited by the Museum's historians and scientists.

While best known for its displays of aircraft, spacecraft, and other exhibits, the Museum also is an internationally recognized research center for the history of aviation and spaceflight and for Earth and planetary science; it maintains collections of objects not on display; and it offers a broad range of public programs and services. Museum staff also raise funds to support new exhibits; work with and provide information to the press and media; maintain an enormously popular website; plan and manage special events; and keep the building clean, safe, and secure.

Behind the Scenes

The core of the Museum is its collections: nearly 30,000 aviation artifacts and 9,000 space artifacts, including more than 350 aircraft and scores of rockets and spacecraft. The collections also comprise engines, propellers, guns, cannons, bombs, bombsights, flight instruments, aerial cameras, uniforms, spacesuits, flight suits, trophies, medals, aviation and space memorabilia, models, space food, scientific instruments, artworks, posters, documents, manuscripts, films, and photographs that document the history of flight. As mind-boggling as the Museum's exhibit halls are, they only display about 10 percent of the collection. Another 10 percent is on loan to museums throughout the United States and in other countries. The rest is on exhibit at the Udvar-Hazy Center or in storage awaiting restoration and display.

Three curatorial and science divisions—Aeronautics, Space History, and the Center for Earth and Planetary Studies (CEPS)—perform research, collect artifacts, and play a leading role in exhibit development. The divisions' staff members assist the many people who make use of the Museum's vast resources, and they answer numerous inquiries and requests from the public on myriad subjects. The historians and scientists in the divisions disseminate their research through books and articles for the general public, scholarly and scientific papers in professional journals, and lectures to the public and professional communities. The divisions also offer fellowships for pre- and postdoctoral and nonacademic researchers.

The Aeronautics Division and the Space History Division preserve, document, and interpret the history of aviation and spaceflight. Aeronautics' research efforts encompass the broad range of technological, military, political, economic, social, and material culture aspects of aviation. Space History focuses on spacecraft and rocketry; human spaceflight; civil, military, and foreign space programs; space science and astronomy; and computers and avionics.

CEPS scientists conduct research in planetary and terrestrial geology and geophysics using remote-sensing data from Earth-orbiting satellites and manned and unmanned space missions. The scope of their research includes Mercury, Venus, the Moon, Mars, asteroids, satellites of the outer solar system, and areas on Earth that shed light on the geological processes of other worlds. CEPS also maintains a vast collection of images of the Earth, Moon, and planets.

The Collections Division is responsible for protecting, preserving, conserving, and restoring the Museum's artifacts. The division is headquartered at the Paul E. Garber Preservation, Restoration, and Storage Facility (the renamed Silver Hill facility) in nearby Maryland, but it will move to the Udvar-Hazy Center when Phase 2 of that facility—with its new restoration hangar—is completed. Collections staff restore aircraft, spacecraft, and other artifacts and prepare them for display. They also process new acquisitions and loans to other institutions and move and install large artifacts for new exhibits.

The Archives Division is responsible for most of the Museum's extensive document, film, and photographic collections relating to the history and technology of aviation and aerospace. Ready reference files, the major photo collections, and the film collection are on the Museum's third floor, along with the Museum's branch of the Smithsonian Libraries. The Garber Facility houses other photo collections and most of the document collections, which include aircraft engineering, technical manuals, manuscript collections, and scrapbooks. These collections will eventually move to the Udvar-Hazy Center. Archives staff answer dozens of inquiries each day from scholars and schoolchildren alike and assist the many researchers who visit the Archives by appointment.

Each exhibition created at the Museum is a broad cooperative effort involving dozens of people in many divisions throughout the Museum. The actual production of an exhibition involves one or more of the curatorial and research divisions and the Exhibits Design and Exhibits Production divisions. Curators, historians, and scientists develop the themes and content, select the artifacts and other objects to be displayed, and write the exhibit text. Exhibits staff manage the project, design the exhibition, edit the exhibit text, fabricate the exhibitry and produce the graphics, and install and maintain the exhibition. The Interactive Media Division develops audiovisual elements and web features for exhibits. Education staff help develop content and manage educational programs related to exhibits. The

Discovery Stations, periodically set up in various galleries, give visitors the opportunity to learn about aviation and spaceflight in a personal, hands-on way.

exhibit graphics, production, and paint shops reside at the Garber Facility. The other units are located in the Museum.

The Museum's Education Division offers educational programs, tours, and demonstrations for Museum visitors; publications geared

toward teachers and students; teacher workshops and cooperative programs with school districts; and family workshops, storytelling programs, family nights, and theme days at the Museum. The division also manages the day-to-day operations of the *How Things Fly* gallery. Education also coordinates the activities of Museum volunteers and student interns, all of whom are

essential to helping the Museum fulfill its mission. Visitor Services Division staff and volunteers manage the Welcome Centers at the Museum and Udvar-Hazy Center. The Museum's docents— knowledgeable, specially trained volunteers—give tours and participate in behind-the-scenes projects.

In its own virtual way, the National Air and Space Museum website—www.nasm.si.edu—is as fascinating to explore as the actual museum. The popular website receives millions of hits each month and is constantly growing and evolving. It provides a wealth of information about visiting the Museum and the Udvar-Hazy Center; about exhibitions, collections, research, educational programs, and news and upcoming events; and about how you can get involved.

All told, some 260 staff members, 500 volunteers and docents, and dozens of student interns carry out the mission of the National Air and Space Museum.

Change and Continuity

Change is always in the air here. The museum you may remember from years ago is different from the one you will find today. Improvements have been made to the building itself: a large glass-enclosed restaurant at the east end of the building, new skylights and

Museum docents share their special expertise on aviation and space with visitors.

window walls, an expanded Museum Store, greater accessibility. Many changes have occurred within the exhibition halls. Every gallery has been updated to some extent, and most older exhibitions have been replaced with newer and better ones, allowing the Museum to explore other topics, present new research, and display more of its collections.

The Museum tries to remain timely as well as historical in nature. Television monitors are wheeled out to show current spacecraft launches. Temporary exhibits highlight significant aerospace events or achievements. Media crews frequently choose the Museum as a site for live broadcasts during special anniversaries or while covering breaking news relevant to aviation or space. The Museum has hosted presidential inaugural balls and many other celebrations. Occasionally it is a place for mourning a tragedy.

But for all the changes and constant activity, much is still the same. The Museum remains the preeminent American institution for memorializing flight, and for collecting, preserving, and presenting aviation and space technology. Visitors are still struck with awe when they enter the Museum's grand entrance hall, *Milestones of Flight,* where the *Spirit of St. Louis,* the Apollo 11 command module *Columbia,* and other icons of flight still reside where they have since 1976. Many people feel a personal connection to the Museum or to particular artifacts within it. What they find here brings back memories, evokes pride, and on occasion elicits passionate criticism—all indications of how strongly they feel about the Museum, how deeply it touches them. Perhaps most important of all, the Museum continues to inspire.

The National Air and Space Museum is a big place, with any number of paths to follow. You could start with the 1903 Wright Flyer, now displayed in its own gallery, then visit *Early Flight* to see the 1909 Wright Military Flyer and watch film footage of it in flight. Or go up to the central balcony for a closer look at the *Spirit of St. Louis,* then turn around to find another airplane flown by Charles Lindbergh and his wife Anne Morrow Lindbergh, as well as other aircraft flown by aviation pioneers of the early decades of flight. Or begin at *Columbia,* then visit a real lunar module resting at the east end of the Museum, then go upstairs to *Apollo to the Moon,* where you can see spacesuits worn on the Moon.

Every artifact at the National Air and Space Museum has a story to tell. This guide gives you a preview of what you'll discover. So turn the page, step inside, and have a look around....

Paul E. Garber

Suspended in the Museum's *Early Flight* gallery is the 1909 Wright Military Flyer, oil-stained and weathered, a refined version of its more famous 1903 predecessor. Aside from its historic status as the world's first military airplane, the 1909 Flyer holds special significance for the Museum for another reason: it ignited the passion of a 10-year-old boy who would have a profound impact on the nation's aeronautical heritage.

On a summer day in 1909, Paul Edward Garber rode the trolleys from his home in Washington, D.C., to Arlington, Virginia, then ran another mile to the grounds of Fort Myer. There Orville Wright was scheduled to demonstrate the airplane he and his brother had built for the U.S. Army Signal Corps. The spectacle of the Flyer in flight literally knocked the boy over. He lay on the ground, amazed and transfixed, as the airplane swept by overhead.

That first direct encounter with aviation left an indelible impression on Garber. A few years later, to his surprise and joy, he rediscovered the 1909 Flyer on display in the Smithsonian's Arts and Industries Building. He returned often to see the airplane that had inspired his interest in flight. On one visit in 1920, he pointed out to a curator that the airplane's control cables were incorrectly installed. Impressed, the curator offered the young man a three-month summer job. Paul Garber stayed with the Smithsonian for 72 years.

For the next half century, the evolution of what would eventually become the National Air and Space Museum was guided by the determined, even heroic efforts of Paul Garber, who progressed from a fixer and builder of exhibits to the keeper of the Smithsonian's aeronautical flame and an airplane collector without peer. Working on his own and with little support, Garber almost single-handedly amassed the finest collection of historic aircraft in the world.

From the Navy he acquired the NC-4, the first airplane to cross the Atlantic. He composed the telegram that would encourage Lindbergh to donate his *Spirit of St. Louis* to the Smithsonian. The Northrop Gamma *Polar Star,* which flew across Antarctica; Wiley Post's Lockheed Vega *Winnie Mae;* the Fokker T-2, the first airplane to fly nonstop across the United States; and the Douglas World Cruiser *Chicago,* which completed the first round-the-world flight, are among the many dozens of airplanes that landed in the Smithsonian's collection thanks to Garber. In 1946 the National Air Museum was established within the Smithsonian, and Garber became its first curator.

When the Wright Flyer was bequeathed to the Smithsonian in 1948, Garber brought it home from England. When the onset of the Korean War forced the urgent relocation of the Museum's huge new collection of World War II aircraft, Garber searched for and acquired land in Silver Hill, Maryland, then managed to get a rudimentary storage facility built there almost for free. The Paul E. Garber Preservation, Restoration, and Storage Facility now honors him with its name.

Although forced by civil service requirements to retire in 1969, Garber stayed on as Historian Emeritus and Ramsey Fellow. Returning to his first aeronautical love, he founded the annual Smithsonian Kite Festival and served as master of ceremonies each year. He remained a fixture at the Museum until his death in 1992 at the age of 93. Without Paul Garber, there might still have been a National Air and Space Museum, but it surely would not have become as historically rich an institution as it is today.

Paul E. Garber with one of the prize artifacts he helped acquire for the Museum.

Milestones *of* Flight

The century was new—the Ford Model T was still the car of the future—when the Wright Flyer rose into the wind and skimmed over the sands of Kitty Hawk, North Carolina, at the speed of a trotting horse. Before mid-century an airplane would fly faster than sound, and a few years later another would rocket through the outer reaches of the atmosphere six times faster yet.

At the height of the Roaring '20s, Charles Lindbergh won international acclaim when he became the first to fly across the Atlantic alone. At century's end, two other pioneers would circle the world without landing, borne not on wings but on winds wafting their balloon.

When Robert Goddard launched his first successful liquid-fuel rocket a year before Lindbergh's flight, rocketry belonged more to the realm of science fiction than science. A few decades later, rockets would lift humans into space and land them on the Moon.

The aircraft and spacecraft representing these and other epic achievements from the first century of flight surround you when you enter this gallery from the National Mall. No other exhibition space in any museum in the world conveys so powerfully how far we have come—and how fast—in the realms of aviation and space or features as many historic icons of flight as this, the National Air and Space Museum's grand entrance hall, *Milestones of Flight*.

On December 17, 1903, the Wright Flyer became the first powered, piloted, heavier-than-air machine to achieve sustained, controlled flight. In 2003, to celebrate the centennial of that event, the Museum moved the 1903 Wright Flyer from its position of honor at the center of *Milestones* and moved it upstairs to its own gallery. Intended as a short-term exhibition, *The Wright Brothers & The Invention of the Aerial Age* proved so popular that it still remains, providing visitors with excellent close-up, eye-level views of the world's first successful airplane.

On May 20, 1927, only 24 years after the Wright brothers' historic flights, Charles Lindbergh took off from Roosevelt Field on Long Island, New York, and headed for Paris, France, in a Ryan-built airplane he named the *Spirit of St. Louis.* He arrived 33½ hours later, greeted by a wildly cheering throng 100,000 strong. Many people had crossed the Atlantic by air before him, but Lindbergh was the first to do it alone, a daring feat that earned him a $25,000 prize and worldwide celebrity. But of far greater consequence was the explosion of enthusiasm, business investment, and government support for aviation sparked by his historic flight.

The **Bell XP-59A Airacomet** may be less familiar than the *Spirit,* but it represents a pivotal technological milestone: the first American jet airplane. Powered by the first U.S. turbojet engine, this test aircraft first flew in October 1942. It helped prove that jet-powered flight was feasible and efficient; indeed, jet aircraft would soon dominate both military and commercial aviation.

Jets offered dramatic increases in speed. But as airplanes approached the speed of sound, or Mach 1, they suffered severe

Above: In the Ryan NYP *Spirit of St. Louis*, Charles Lindbergh became the first person to fly alone nonstop across the Atlantic.

Below: Flying the Bell X-1, Chuck Yeager smashed through the mythical "sound barrier" for the first time, reaching a speed of Mach 1.06.

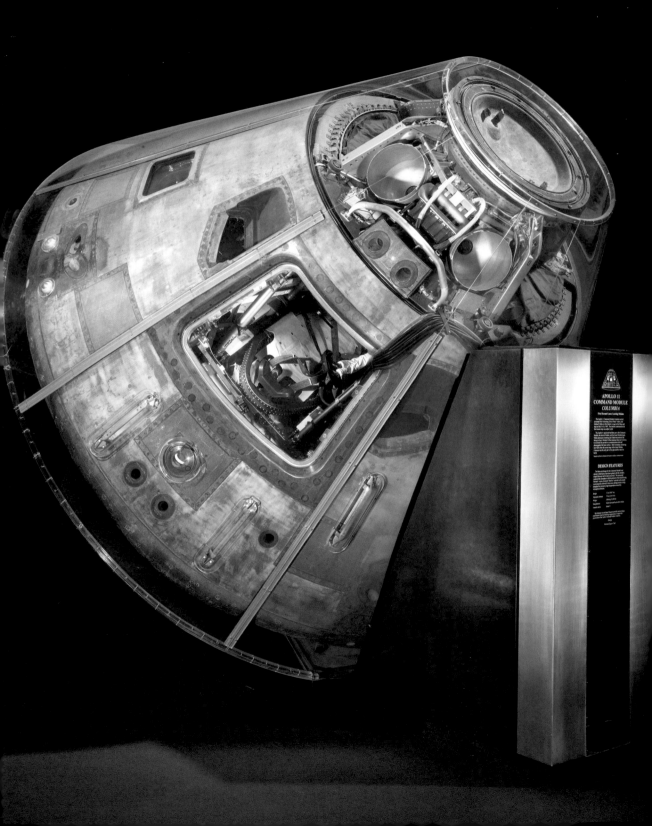

vibration and loss of control, leading many to believe that aircraft could not fly faster than sound. Charles E. "Chuck" Yeager proved them wrong on October 14, 1947, when he pierced the mythical "sound barrier" for the first time in the rocket-powered **Bell X-1** *Glamorous Glennis.* Air-launched from the bomb bay of a Boeing B-29, the bullet-shaped X-1 flew 78 times, once as fast as Mach 1.45.

Other aircraft continued to extend the limits of performance. First flown in 1959, the rocket-powered **North American X-15,** the first of three built, represents the ultimate speed machine. The X-15s exceeded four, five, and six times the speed of sound. One reached Mach 6.72—4,534 miles per hour. No aircraft has ever flown faster. Another flew higher than 67 miles, through the outer reaches of the atmosphere.

Rockets powered by dry chemicals, such as gunpowder, have been around since at least the 13th century. But liquid-fuel rockets were first developed in the early 20th century by rocketry pioneer Robert H. Goddard. Three **Goddard rockets** are on display here: a replica of the world's first liquid-fuel rocket, which he built and launched in March 1926; the oldest surviving liquid-fuel rocket (containing parts from that earlier rocket), which he tried but failed to launch in May 1926; and a P-series rocket, one of his last and most advanced, flown in 1940 and '41. Goddard's technological influence on later rocketry was minimal. But he was among the first to prove that space travel by rocket was feasible, and the impact of this idea on the world's imagination was profound.

The two other rockets in the gallery represent not a milestone of technology, but a milestone in the effort by the United States and the Soviet Union to control nuclear arms. The U.S. **Pershing II** and Soviet **SS-20** missiles were two key weapons banned in 1987 by the

In 1962 John Glenn became the first American to orbit the Earth in this Mercury spacecraft he named *Friendship 7.*

Opposite: The Apollo 11 command module *Columbia* carried astronauts Armstrong, Aldrin, and Collins to the Moon and back in 1969. During that historic mission, Armstrong and Aldrin became the first humans to walk upon the surface of another world.

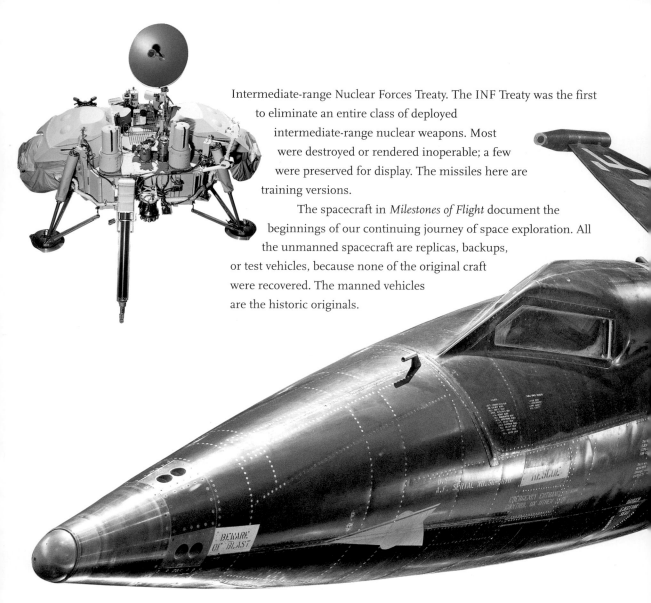

Intermediate-range Nuclear Forces Treaty. The INF Treaty was the first to eliminate an entire class of deployed intermediate-range nuclear weapons. Most were destroyed or rendered inoperable; a few were preserved for display. The missiles here are training versions.

The spacecraft in *Milestones of Flight* document the beginnings of our continuing journey of space exploration. All the unmanned spacecraft are replicas, backups, or test vehicles, because none of the original craft were recovered. The manned vehicles are the historic originals.

This Viking lander is similar to the two spacecraft that soft-landed on Mars in 1976 and sent back the first images and data from the surface.

The Soviet Union's launch of **Sputnik 1**, the world's first artificial satellite, on October 4, 1957, took America by surprise and signaled the start of the Space Race. On January 31, 1958, the United States responded by launching **Explorer 1**, which along with Explorer 3 found evidence of radiation belts surrounding the Earth, the first major scientific discovery of the space age. The launching of humans into space soon followed, with the Soviets leading the way. In 1961 President John F. Kennedy raised the stakes of the Space Race by challenging America to land a man on the Moon before the end of the decade.

The next few years saw many spectacular achievements. On February 20, 1962, John Glenn became the first American to orbit the

Earth in his Mercury spacecraft *Friendship 7.* Glenn circled the globe three times during his five-hour flight, before splashing down in the Atlantic. His success boosted American confidence that the United States could compete with—and perhaps beat—the Soviet Union in the Space Race.

A series of two-man Gemini spacecraft tested rendezvous and docking techniques and the effects on astronauts of prolonged stays in space. On June 3, 1965, **Gemini IV** carried astronauts Edward White and James McDivitt into orbit, and a few hours later White became the first American to "walk" in space. He remained outside for about 20 minutes, tethered to the spacecraft by a long cord and using a handheld jet thruster to move about.

The **Apollo 11 command module** *Columbia* represents a profoundly significant milestone: the first time humans set foot on another world. *Columbia* carried astronauts Neil Armstrong, Edwin "Buzz" Aldrin, and Michael Collins to lunar orbit. From there Armstrong and Aldrin began their final descent in the lunar module *Eagle.* On July 20, 1969, people around the world heard the first words transmitted from the lunar surface: "Houston, Tranquility Base here. The *Eagle* has landed." Hours later, Armstrong and then Aldrin stepped down onto the Moon. They later rejoined Collins in *Columbia,* the only part of the Apollo 11 spacecraft to return to Earth.

While the race to the Moon was taking place, robotic exploration of the solar system was beginning. In 1962 **Mariner 2** flew past Venus

The rocket-powered North American X-15 is the fastest type of aircraft ever flown. One of the three X-15s exceeded six times the speed of sound.

and returned scientific data on the surface temperature and environment of Earth's nearest planetary neighbor—the first successful mission to another planet. **Pioneer 10** was the first spacecraft to traverse the outer solar system. After passing through the asteroid belt, it sent back the first close-up images of Jupiter in 1973. Ten years later, Pioneer 10 became the first craft to reach a distance beyond all known planets. The **Viking** lander is similar to the two spacecraft that in 1976 became the first to land on Mars. The Vikings studied the Martian surface and atmosphere and analyzed the soil, searching for—but not finding—organic compounds or other traces of life.

In the **Breitling Orbiter 3** gondola, pilots Bertrand Piccard and Brian Jones became the first to fly nonstop around the world in a balloon. Their flight in March 1999 began with their ascent from a Swiss Alpine village and ended 20 days later in the Egyptian desert. As the 1900s ended, the flight of Piccard and Jones marked the last great milestone of the first century of flight.

The second century of flight opened with its own milestone. On June 21, 2004, air-launched from a custom-designed mother ship, the rocket-powered **SpaceShipOne** briefly ascended just beyond the atmosphere and then glided back to Earth to become the first privately

The *Milestones of Flight gallery.*

Opposite: In the Breitling Orbiter 3, pilots Bertrand Piccard and Brian Jones became the first to fly nonstop around the world by balloon. Their flight in 1999 lasted 20 days.

developed, piloted vehicle to reach space. Designed by innovative aeronautical engineer Burt Rutan, SpaceShipOne repeated that achievement two more times in the following months to win the $10-million Ansari X Prize for repeated flights in a privately developed reusable spacecraft. The dream of affordable, commercial spaceflight was one small step closer.

Small treasures and other attractions:

Don't miss the opportunity to touch a piece of an actual Moon rock brought back to Earth by Apollo 17 astronauts in 1972.

Above: The *Milestones of Flight* gallery.

Below: SpaceShipOne, the first privately developed, piloted vehicle to reach space.

Opposite: In *Milestones of Flight* you can touch a piece of a Moon rock brought back to Earth by Apollo 17 astronauts.

Right: The Soviet SS-20 (left) and U.S. Pershing II missiles were among the nuclear weapons eliminated by the landmark Intermediate-range Nuclear Forces Treaty in 1987.

Far Right: The *Milestones of Flight* gallery.

AVIATION

The *America by Air* gallery.

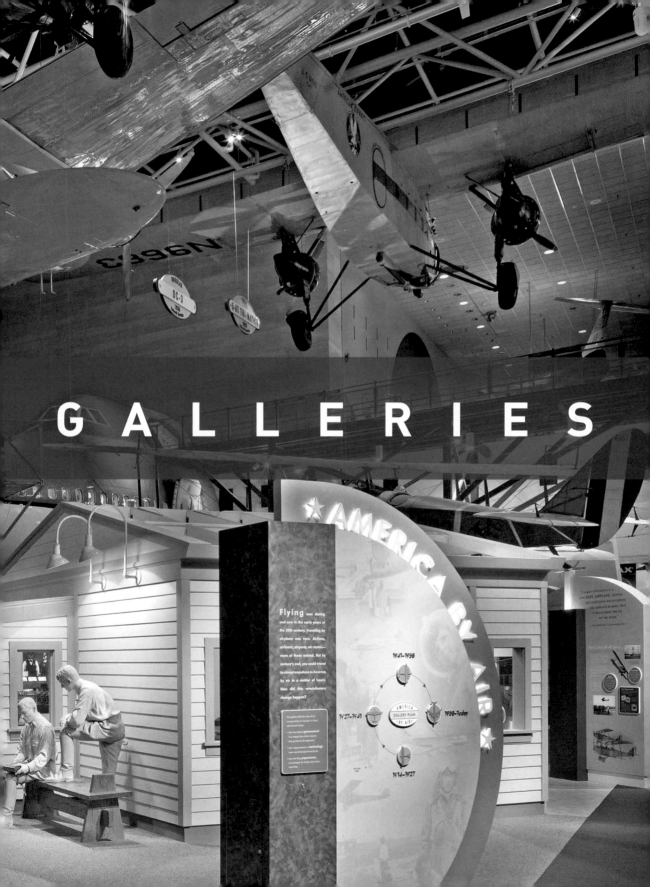

GALLERIES

America by Air

O n New Year's Day 1914, a flying boat crossed Florida's Tampa Bay carrying a paying passenger. The trip took 23 minutes—11 hours less than by train—and inaugurated something new in American life: scheduled airline service. The St. Petersburg–Tampa Airboat Line lasted only three months, but in that time it transported 1,204 passengers across the bay. It would be a while before most people would trust airplanes enough to consider traveling in one; longer before transporting people would become economical for airlines; still longer before air travel would become inexpensive enough for most Americans to afford.

In *America by Air* you can see, in one sweeping glance, what that modest beginning led to in the decades that followed. Represented among the gallery's constellation of airplanes are many of the great names—Eastern, United, American, TWA, Pan Am, Northwest—and some of the most important aircraft from the airline industry's formative years.

The exhibition traces the history of air transportation in four chronological sections: "The Early Years of Air Transportation," "Airline Expansion and Innovation," "The Heyday of Propeller Airlines," and "The Jet Age." Three themes weave through all these sections: how the federal government has shaped the airline industry, how improvements in technology have revolutionized air travel, and how the flying experience has changed.

Like other early airlines, the St. Petersburg–Tampa Airboat Line failed because transporting passengers was not yet profitable. But airlines did find success in another role: carrying the mail. The U.S. Post Office began flying mail after World War I and eventually turned the task over to commercial airlines. Designed as a trainer for the U.S. Army Air Service during World War I, the **Curtiss JN-4D Jenny** was the

first aircraft used in regular service by the Post Office. Also widely flown by traveling exhibition flyers called barnstormers, the Jenny was the first airplane many people ever saw. The one displayed here, a rare and fragile treasure, was acquired by the Smithsonian in 1918.

Gradually, the federal government established an expanding system of airline routes. The **Pitcairn PA-5 Mailwing** was designed for eastern U.S. air mail routes and flown by Eastern Air Transport (later Eastern Air Lines). The Mailwing had a Wright Whirlwind engine, more reliable and efficient and much lighter in weight than the Jenny's World War I–era Liberty engine.

The **Fairchild FC-2** was designed for aerial photography by Sherman Fairchild. He wanted an airplane that could provide a wide field of view, was stable and roomy, and had an enclosed cabin, so he created the airplane he needed. FC-2s were also used to fly air mail, passengers, and freight. Pan American–Grace Airways flew the one displayed here in the late 1920s in South America.

This rare vintage Curtiss JN-4D Jenny represents the first type of aircraft used in regular service by the U.S. Post Office. Many barnstormers flew Jennys as well.

Overleaf: *America by Air* explores the history of air transportation from the early days of air mail flights through modern jet travel.

But for passenger air travel to really take off, airlines needed a bigger, more reliable, more economical airplane—and one that people trusted. Enter Henry Ford, the man who put America on wheels. Ford's foray into the aircraft business was brief but pivotal. In 1925 the company introduced a series of airliners that culminated in the **Ford 5-AT Tri-Motor.** The largest American airliner of its day, it could carry up to 15 passengers. Its three engines, all-metal construction, and corrugated aluminum skin made it strong, durable, and reliable. But most important was the prestigious Ford name. The confidence people

had in Ford automobiles carried over to Ford airplanes. The "Tin Goose" was terribly noisy and not terribly fast, and flying remained too expensive for most people, but the Tri-Motor helped convince the public that air travel was safe and practical.

The sleek **Northrop Alpha** represents a transitional design, innovative yet curiously anachronistic. Introduced in 1930 by the ingenious Jack Northrop, the streamlined, all-metal airplane was

The Ford 5-AT Tri-Motor helped build public confidence in air travel. The largest American airliner of its day, it could carry up to 15 passengers.

designed to carry both mail and passengers in and out of small airfields. It could accommodate six people in a snug, enclosed cabin, and its structural design would help shape the next generation of airliners. But the Alpha also maintained older features: fixed landing gear, a single engine, and an open cockpit that exposed the pilot to the elements—still considered by many to be an essential aspect of flying.

The first truly modern airliner appeared in 1933. The Boeing 247 featured cantilevered wings; all-metal, stressed-skin construction; a pair of engines built into the wings; and retractable landing gear. The **Boeing 247-D** hanging here also introduced controllable-pitch propellers and wing deicers. The 247 provided a new level of comfort for its complement of 10 passengers: soundproofing, low vibration,

and plush seats. It revolutionized air transportation, cutting cross-country travel time and rendering its competition obsolete.

The group of carriers that would form United Air Lines monopolized production orders for 247s, forcing other airlines to turn to Douglas Aircraft for a competitive airliner. Douglas countered with the DC-2. Then in 1935 it introduced the Douglas Sleeper-Transport, or DST, a larger airplane with 14 comfortable sleeping berths for overnight transcontinental flights. The day version of the aircraft was designated the **Douglas DC-3**. The impact of the DC-3 can hardly be overstated. It was faster and more luxurious and could seat twice as many passengers as the Boeing 247. Its speed, efficiency, and capacity

The Douglas DC-3 revolutionized air travel in the 1930s. This DC-3 flew for Eastern Air Lines from 1937 to 1952.

made it the first airplane that could turn a profit by carrying only passengers. It quickly dominated airline routes in the United States and around the world. Military versions carried troops and cargo in World War II.

After the war, what many people nostalgically think of as the

golden age of air travel began. Bigger and faster airliners cut travel times and made air travel cheaper and more comfortable. With airfares regulated, airlines competed by offering better service. Air travel was still a luxury for most people, but by the mid-1950s more Americans were traveling by air than by train, and airliners began to supersede ocean liners for transatlantic travel. The nose section of the American Airlines **Douglas DC-7** *Flagship Vermont* represents the last generation of the great propeller-driven airliners. You can take a look inside for a sense of that bygone era. The four-engine DC-7 was the fastest airliner when introduced in 1953 and the first that could fly nonstop across the country in either direction.

The introduction of jetliners in the late 1950s, beginning with the Boeing 707 and Douglas DC-8 in the United States, ended the dominance of propeller-driven airliners. In the 1970s, the first generation of wide-body jetliners equipped with fuel-efficient, high-bypass turbofan engines entered service, led by the huge **Boeing 747.** The nose section of a Northwest Airlines 747 dominates one side of the gallery. You can enter its upper deck from the Museum's second floor.

Such technologically advanced aircraft and the deregulation of the airline industry in the late 1970s transformed air travel and brought airline tickets within the economic reach of most people. In the following decades, digital technology revolutionized everything from cockpit controls to airline reservations and ticketing. Terrorism reshaped airline security and the travel experience. The romance of air travel has faded, but in its place is a safe and affordable air transportation network that binds together the nation and the world.

The Douglas DC-7 airliner cabin offered ample leg room, window curtains, and limited overhead storage.

Opposite: The nose section of a Northwest Airlines Boeing 747 jetliner protrudes from one wall of the gallery. You can enter the aircraft's upper deck from a bridge on the Museum's second floor.

Small treasures and other attractions:

You can also examine vintage flight crew uniforms, air travel
memorabilia, airliner models, and aircraft engines. Don't miss the
"stand-on" exhibit that demonstrates how it felt to fly in a Ford Tri-
Motor, the touchable luggage pile that reveals how much we rely on air
transportation, and the exhibit comparing flying "Then and Now." A
simulated Airbus A320 cockpit and display provides a 360-degree view
of a landing and takeoff. A computer animation in the Air Traffic
Control section shows air traffic over the United States on a typical day,
during a major weather event, and on September 11, 2001.

You can enter the nose section of
the American Airlines Douglas
DC-7 *Flagship Vermont*—and find
out what it took to become an airline
stewardess in the 1950s.

Opposite Above: You can poke
around in a pile of luggage
beneath the Boeing 747 to discover
some of the many ways that air
transportation affects our lives.

Opposite Below: The simulated
cockpit of an Airbus A320 illustrates
digital "fly-by-wire" technology
through a takeoff and landing at a
nearby airport.

The Wright Brothers
& THE INVENTION OF THE AERIAL AGE

On December 17, 1903, on a windswept beach at Kitty Hawk, North Carolina, Orville and Wilbur Wright made four sustained, controlled flights aboard a heavier-than-air, powered aircraft. The first flight lasted 12 seconds; the last and longest flight lasted almost a minute. The 1903 Wright Flyer never flew again after that day, but those first brief flights proved that humanity's ancient dreams of flight could really be achieved.

How these two brothers from Dayton, Ohio, reached this epic technological milestone, and the impact their invention had on the world of the early 20th century, is a story not widely known among today's harried air travelers. To celebrate the 100th anniversary of their historic flights, in 2003 the National Air and Space Museum moved the Wright Flyer from its place of honor at the center of the *Milestones of Flight* gallery to its own exhibition space, where it could be viewed close-up at eye level, and where its story and that of its creators could be fully told.

The Wright Brothers & The Invention of the Aerial Age tells that story in three parts. The first section focuses on the Wright brothers themselves: who they were and what they were like, the influences their family and environment had on them, and their early careers as printers and bicycle builders in Dayton, Ohio. On display are printing type and blocks they used in their printing business, examples of pamphlets and newspapers they produced, Orville's mandolin, and a Wright-designed and -built St. Clair bicycle, one of only five bicycles manufactured by the Wright brothers known to exist.

The second and largest section explores their years of methodical aeronautical research and experimentation that culminated in the first successful airplane. The Wright brothers accomplished three key

things. They designed, built, and flew a series of aircraft. They pioneered the basic approach and techniques of modern aeronautical engineering, including the use of a wind tunnel as a key design tool. And they developed and refined their designs based on a systematic program of flight testing. They continued refining their airplane design after 1903, finally perfecting it two years later.

Reproductions of three early craft the Wright brothers built to test their design ideas hang in the open gallery space, surrounded by murals and architectural facades. With their **1899 Wright Kite**, a biplane-type design with a five-foot wingspan, they tested their control system. The **1900 Wright Glider,** their first piloted aircraft, incorporated the wire-braced biplane structure and wing-warping and pitch control system they developed with the kite. The control system worked well, but the glider generated less lift than expected. Their next aircraft, their 1901 glider, proved to be a discouraging— but instructive—setback. The glider had a longer wing span and more curved airfoil, but it performed worse than their previous one and still lacked enough lift.

The Wrights decided to obtain their own lift and drag data using a wind tunnel, rather than relying on the data of others, and that decision

To celebrate the 100th anniversary of the Wright brothers' historic flights, the Wright Flyer was relocated from *Milestones of Flight* to the center of this gallery, where you can now examine the airplane close-up at eye level.

Following pages: Captured at the moment of takeoff on its historic first flight, the 1903 Wright Flyer lifts into the air above the launch rail that served as its runway. Orville is at the controls; Wilbur stands at the right.

proved to be a turning point in their aeronautical research. The aircraft that resulted, the 1902 **Wright Glider,** was a breakthrough. They had finally resolved the lift problem and created the world's first fully controllable aircraft.

Resting on the floor at the center of the gallery, visible from all sides, is the ultimate product of their years of careful work. The 1903 **Wright Flyer** is the real thing: the first powered, piloted, heavier-than-air machine to achieve sustained, controlled flight—the world's first successful airplane. On its first flight it traveled 120 feet, and on its last flight it covered 852 feet, roughly the length of the Museum. The aerial age had begun.

The exhibition includes many historic photographs and cultural artifacts, along with instruments and personal items associated with the Wrights. You can examine a wing tip—the only surviving piece—from their 1902 glider, a launching dolly from 1909 similar to the one they used in 1903, wind tunnel balances and models they used during testing, and tools that belonged to their assistant, Charlie Taylor, the mechanic who helped designed and build the engine for

Wilbur and Orville Wright designed and built this St. Clair bicycle, one of only five bicycles manufactured by the brothers that still exist.

Opposite: The Wright brothers began devoting their technical skill and engineering genius to the challenge of human flight in the late 1890s. After years of careful research and testing, they built and flew the world's first successful airplane.

the Wright Flyer. Hands-on exhibits showing structural elements and demonstrating how they worked provide an engaging way to learn about the airplane's technical features. Computer programs enable you to explore the airplane's components and view simulations of its flights.

The third and final section of the gallery reveals how the world reacted to the Wright brothers' invention—once they chose to reveal it—in the years that followed, and its wide-ranging influence from popular culture to military planning. After their triumph at Kitty Hawk, the Wrights quietly continued to refine their invention. They did not publicly promote their airplane until 1908, when they embarked upon demonstration tours in the United States and Europe.

The effect of those demonstrations was immediate and profound. Orville and Wilbur became international celebrities, and people everywhere became fascinated with airplanes and intrigued by their potential. Art, literature, music, and popular culture began to reflect flight's growing popularity. You can view film clips and artwork, listen to musical scores, and examine memorabilia and posters from air meets. Flying exhibitions and competitions emerged. Aviators became the century's first celebrities. Journalists, politicians, and military strategists began to debate and influence aviation's future.

The Wright brothers used this stopwatch to time their historic first flights on December 17, 1903.

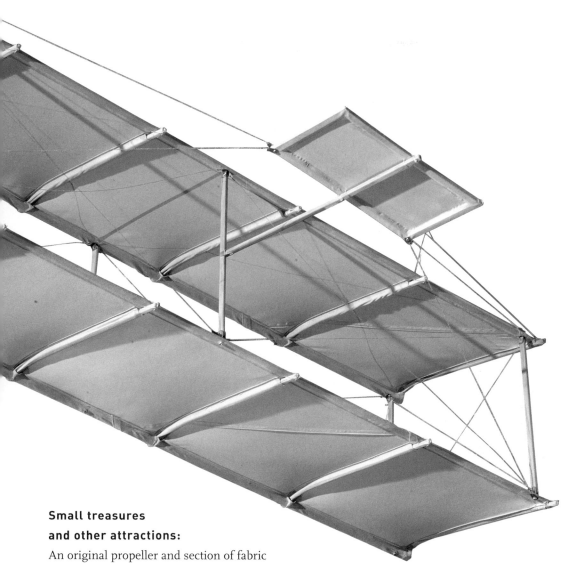

Small treasures
and other attractions:

An original propeller and section of fabric
from the Wright Flyer is on display (the aircraft has
been restored twice over the years), along with a stopwatch
and pocket watch used by Orville and Wilbur on the day of their
historic flights. You can watch actual film footage of their 1909
Wright Military Flyer—the world's first military airplane—during its
flight trials at Fort Myer, Virginia.

The Wright brothers began their
program of flight testing in 1899
with a kite. The gallery displays
reproductions of the kite (shown
here) and two of the gliders they
built on their way to creating their
1903 Flyer.

Early Flight

Word of the Wright brothers' success quietly rippled outward in the years following their historic flights of December 1903. The news reinvigorated the efforts of other aerial pioneers, especially in Europe. Other fledgling flyers soon managed to get airborne, but the performance of their aircraft was so limited that the rumored achievements of the Wright brothers seemed hard to believe.

The Wrights continued to improve their airplane while guarding its technical details. Orville and Wilbur finally began publicly demonstrating their invention in 1908 and 1909 in Europe and America. Their sustained, controlled flights astounded onlookers and sparked an explosion of enthusiasm for aviation. Within ten years after those first flights at Kitty Hawk, the world had found its wings and the age of flight had truly begun.

The *Samuel P. Langley Gallery of Early Flight* celebrates that first decade of flight by evoking the atmosphere of an aviation exhibition from that period: the fictitious Smithsonian Aeronautical Exposition of 1913. The gaily decorated gallery is crammed with fabric-covered aerial vehicles, some fanciful, most real, along with trade show–style exhibits featuring cutting-edge technology of the day.

The Exposition entrance area offers a glance back at how the ancient dream of flight evolved and at some of the concepts for flying machines developed over the centuries. An important influence on the Wrights was Otto Lilienthal, a German glider pioneer who spent decades studying bird flight and developing man-carrying gliders. From 1891 until his death from a flying accident in 1896, he made about 2,000 glider flights. Hanging here is a rare **1894 Lilienthal glider,** the type he considered his safest and most successful.

Secretary of the Smithsonian Samuel P. Langley was also keenly interested in heavier-than-air flight. In 1896 **Langley's Aerodrome #5** made the first successful flight of an engine-driven, heavier-than-air craft of substantial size. The unmanned craft flew about half a mile on its longest flight. Also hanging here is **Langley's Quarter-Scale**

Aerodrome, a successfully flown scale model of a piloted aircraft. Langley finally created a full-scale piloted aircraft, the Aerodrome A, and tested it in late 1903, only weeks before the Wright brothers' historic flights. But in two launch attempts from a catapult atop a houseboat, the "Great Aerodrome" merely plunged into the Potomac River. The engine that powered the ill-fated aircraft is on display.

But the Exposition doesn't dwell on tragedy and failure; it celebrates success and progress. Hanging here is the most original and complete of the Museum's three Wright airplanes, the **1909 Wright Military Flyer.** The Wright brothers built it to fulfill a request by the U.S. Army Signal Corps for a two-seat observation aircraft. Orville Wright began the demonstration trials in 1908 at Fort Myer, Virginia, just across the river from Washington, D.C., in an earlier version of this airplane. But it crashed, seriously injuring Orville Wright and killing his passenger. In 1909 Orville continued the trials in this airplane. It exceeded performance requirements and the Army purchased it, making this craft the world's first military airplane.

An exhibit on the Wright Company airplane factory in Dayton, Ohio, has models showing how early Wright airplane designs evolved, a wind gauge the brothers used at Kitty Hawk, a Wright engine from

The glider flights of German aeronautical pioneer Otto Lilienthal inspired the Wright brothers to pursue the challenge of flight. This 1894 glider is one of only six Lilienthal gliders still in existence.

Glenn Curtiss used this motorcycle to test an airplane engine at Ormond Beach, Florida, in 1907. On a trial run, he set a land speed record of 136 miles per hour.

Opposite Above: Many famous exhibition flyers flew the Curtiss Model D "Headless Pusher," because it was very maneuverable and could easily be taken apart, shipped, and reassembled at the next venue.

Opposite Below: Developed for the U.S. Army, the 1909 Wright Military Flyer was the world's first military airplane. While similar in design to the 1903 Wright Flyer, it could fly much farther and longer.

1913, and a reproduction of the wind tunnel they built in 1901 and used to conduct aerodynamic research critical to their success.

Adjacent is a display of the rival Curtiss Aeroplane Company of Hammondsport, New York. A former bicycle builder like the Wrights, Glenn Curtiss made a name for himself building motorcycles and engines. On display is a motorcycle he used to test a V-8 airplane engine. On a trial run in 1907 at Ormond Beach, Florida, Curtiss reached a record speed of 136 miles per hour, a feat for which he became known as the "fastest man on earth." Displayed above is a Curtiss Model D "Headless Pusher," a 1912 design and the standard airplane flown by the Curtiss exhibition team. The airplane is so named because the forward elevator (found on such airplanes as the Wright Flyer) has been removed, and because the propellers push, rather than pull, the airplane.

Countless other daring and unsung aviation pioneers built airplanes in their backyards from materials purchased from local hardware stores. In 1912 or '13, Herman Ecker of Syracuse, New York, constructed the **Ecker Flying Boat** displayed here. He patterned it after a Curtiss design and improvised as needed. Displayed with its streamlined boat hull, the airplane at other times was equipped with

wheeled landing gear and pontoons.

Despite the success of the Wrights and Curtiss, Europe had become the center of aeronautical activity and innovation. In 1909 Frenchman Louis Blériot achieved the momentous feat of crossing the English Channel in an earlier version of the **Blériot XI** exhibited here. This Blériot was owned by Swiss aviator John Domenjoz, who emblazoned his name on the wing and flew the airplane in aerial exhibitions in Europe, the United States, and South America. You can perceive the future of the airplane beginning to emerge in the Blériot's design: a single rather than a double wing, wheels rather than runners, the pilot seated within a fuselage, and horizontal and vertical control surfaces at the tail.

Other exhibits feature less-known and soon-to-be-known aviators from many nations and their flying machines, pioneering women aviators, early aircraft engines, and posters, programs, and photos from some of the great aviation meets that brought the thrilling new spectacle of flight to people around the world.

Small treasures and other attractions:
Glenn Curtiss's pilot's license, issued by the Aero Club of America on June 8, 1911, is displayed near his motorcycle. "The Aeroplane: A Chronicle of Flight in Moving Pictures" presents vintage film footage of aerial expositions, a Curtiss Headless Pusher racing Eddie Rickenbacker's race car, the Wright Military Flyer in its trial flights at Fort Myer, and the first film footage taken from an airplane.

Oppsite Above: Louis Blériot's daring crossing of the English Channel in 1909 in a Blériot XI made these single-wing airplanes popular among European aviators. This one was owned by Swiss stunt pilot John Domenjoz.

Oppsite Below: Pilot Herman Ecker built this homemade flying boat in the early 1900s, basing it on a Curtiss design. A six-cylinder marine engine converted for aeronautical use powered the airplane.

Legend, Memory,
& THE GREAT WAR IN THE AIR

In the years since World War I, popular culture has distilled that distant conflict down to a few memorable images. One is of waves of soldiers being slaughtered by machine-gun fire as they go "over the top" of their muddy trenches into "no-man's-land." Another is of gallant fighter pilots dueling in the skies above, where combat was ruled by a code of honor, victory brought glory, and death came quickly and cleanly.

The first image is tragically accurate. The other is misleading, for it ignores the realities of flying: the poor training, inadequate equipment, brutality of combat, and short life expectancy of pilots. It also implies that aviators, especially aces, played a more crucial role in the war than they really did. Notions of fighter pilots as chivalrous "knights of the sky" have imbued our remembrance of the air war with a soft, romantic glow. *Legend, Memory, and the Great War in the Air* reexamines aviation during World War I and contrasts that romance with reality.

Near the entrance are relatively recent cultural artifacts relating to the war: games, models, comic books, paperbacks, and depictions of America's favorite World War I flyer, Snoopy, who through clenched teeth mutters "Curse you, Red Baron!" at his nemesis. Nearby is an exhibit on the real Red Baron, Manfred von Richthofen. An ace with 80 victories, he was a national hero in Germany at the time he died in combat. A child's room from the 1930s, filled with toys, models, and books relating to the war, hints at the impact on popular culture in the postwar years.

Hollywood films played the greatest role in shaping people's perceptions of the air war. A theater presents clips from several films from the 1920s and '30s that romanticized aviators and aerial combat. Above the theater hangs a colorful German **Pfalz D.XII**, an airplane

that logged more hours in Hollywood movies than in combat. With its fictitious red paint scheme and skull-and-crossbones insignia, it appears as it did in the 1930 film *The Dawn Patrol.*

Beyond the theater you confront the war's grim reality: a trench diorama featuring a large, graphic image of a rotting corpse and footage from *All Quiet on the Western Front,* the film from the postwar era that came closest to capturing the war's horror and futility. The central reality of World War I was not dueling aces, but trench warfare. Within a year after it began in 1914, the war had spread like cancer beyond reason or control. A labyrinth of trenches hundreds of miles long scarred central Europe. The fighting had degenerated into a bloody stalemate and was inflicting staggering losses.

The airplane's impact on the war's outcome was limited, but it did play a decisive role in some early battles when used for observing and tracking enemy forces. Battlefield strategists began experimenting with other uses, and industry began producing airplanes designed for those new roles. The airplanes in this gallery—many of them extremely rare—along with dioramas, models, engines, and other artifacts, illustrate the successes and failures of these efforts.

Germany's best fighter, the Fokker D.VII. This plane was captured two days before the Armistice, when its pilot mistakenly landed at an American airfield.

Pilot Ray Brooks named this French SPAD XIII *Smith IV*, after his fiancée's college. Painted on the lower-right fuselage is a row of tombstones, one for every mission on which Brooks cheated death. Iron Cross emblems cover many bullet holes that testify to how close death often came. Brooks lived to see his airplane displayed in the Museum.

Opposite Above: This French Voisin VIII was one of the world's first bombers. The pilot aimed with a bombsight through glass panels in the nose, then released the bombs from trapdoors in the fuselage floor.

Opposite Below: Germany's Red Baron, Manfred von Richthofen, scored most of his 80 victories in Albatros fighters. This model D.Va is one of only two Albatros aircraft left in the world.

The necessities of war accelerated aircraft development. With its behind-the-wing pusher propeller, the British Royal Aircraft Factory F.E.8 (a fuselage replica is on display) was state-of-the-art when unveiled in 1915. But by the time it reached the battlefield, it was already an easy kill for better warplanes. Other aircraft were more successful. Fast, rugged, and well-armed, the French **SPAD XIII** was one of the war's best fighters. Pilots of many Allied nations, including most American pilots, flew SPADs late in the war. The airplane displayed here is one of only four left.

The United States had only 50 outdated military airplanes when it entered the war in 1917. Still, America promised to fill the skies of Europe with swarms of British-designed de Havilland DH-4 "Liberty Planes," which were to roll off U.S. assembly lines like Ford Model Ts. However, mass production of DH-4s proved problematic. America's manpower, not its limited air power, would break the stalemate in Europe.

Germany struggled with its own problems: dealing with shortages of skilled labor and aircraft-quality materials, and finding ways to

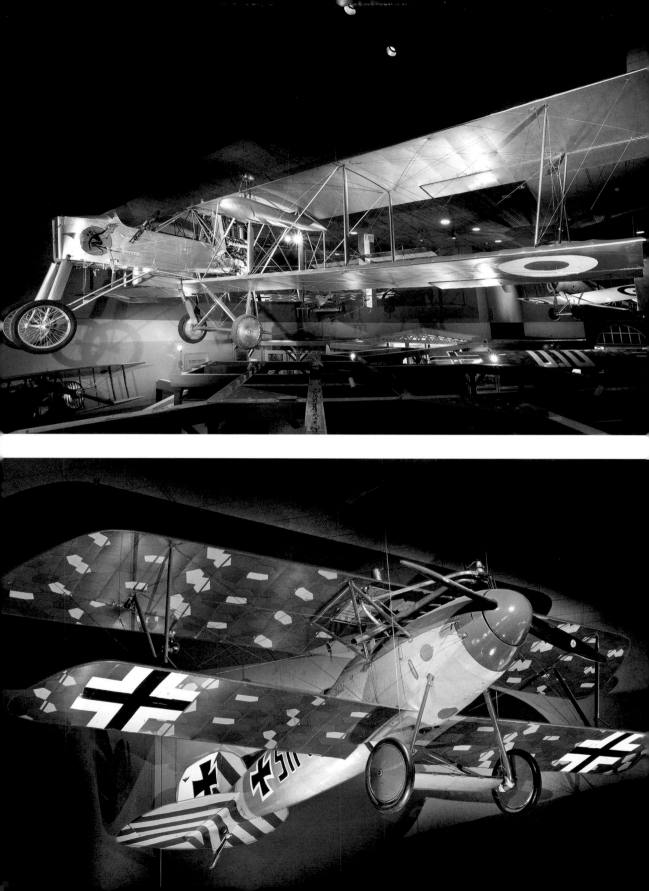

improve airplanes without slowing production. The **Albatros D.Va** exemplifies the compromises that sometimes had to be made. To compensate for design flaws and production difficulties, German crews in the field had to modify each new Albatros before it could be safely flown. The airplane exhibited here is one of only two Albatros aircraft of any version that survive.

Germany had its best success with the **Fokker D.VII.** Innovative construction techniques made the airplane strong, fast, and easy to maintain. Introduced late in the war, these aircraft became so feared and respected that the terms of the Armistice specifically required Germany to surrender all of them to the Allies.

The airplane's most ominous new role was strategic bombing—attacking cities and industries from the air. For the first time, civilian populations fell under aerial attack. On display is the only surviving **Sopwith 7F.1 Snipe**, a British fighter that made its appearance late in the war. The big French **Voisin VIII** is the type of bomber that carried

Britain developed the Sopwith Snipe late in the war to replace its Sopwith Camel. The Snipe hanging in the gallery is the only survivor of its type.

out the first nighttime attacks against towns and factories in Germany.

The airplane was a largely untested weapon when World War I began. By war's end in 1918, air forces had grown enormously, aviation had become highly organized, and a heritage of military aviation had been born. The image of the fighter pilot as a glamorous hero had gripped the public imagination—a hold it has yet to release.

Small treasures and other attractions:

An exhibit on the hazards of flying includes the personal effects of a British airman. Nearby is a machine gun recovered from a crashed German airplane, its bent muzzle still clogged with soil from the Verdun battlefield. A video featuring Ray Brooks, who flew the SPAD XIII displayed in this gallery, presents his firsthand experiences of the war in the air.

A German aircraft factory diorama illustrates the industrial pressures Germany faced late in the war. Women and sailors were enlisted to work, and due to rubber shortages, women were encouraged to donate their hair to be made into machinery drive belts.

The Golden Age of Flight

Two colorful airplanes hanging from the ceiling draw your attention when you enter this gallery. But don't overlook the smaller things here, for they tell a big story. Newspaper headlines on the walls boldly proclaim, "400,000 See Pageant Open Air Races," "U.S. Air Record Smashed by Turner," "Lindbergh Does It!" Movie posters advertise *Wings of Glory* and *Flight from Glory*. Models of airplanes, some three dozen in all, range in style from the barnstorming Jenny to a B-17 bomber, from the stubby Gee-Bee racer to the elegant, gull-winged Stinson Reliant. Photos and magazine covers capture heroes of the day: Jimmy Doolittle, Jackie Cochran, Amelia Earhart, Howard Hughes, Roscoe Turner. Air-racing trophies depict streamlined, winged human forms rising toward the sky or streaking toward the finish line, toward an air-minded future.

Americans were wild about aviation in the 1920s and '30s, the period between the two world wars that came to be known as the Golden Age of Flight. Air races and daring record-setting flights dominated the news. Airplanes evolved from wood-and-fabric biplanes to streamlined metal monoplanes. The military services embraced air power. Aviation came of age. *The Golden Age of Flight* gallery focuses on this dynamic period.

Air races and air shows were hugely popular, and many men and women fliers became household names. Trophies for which they competed are on display, including the prestigious Thompson and Bendix trophies. Hanging near the gallery entrance is the **Wittman *Buster***, a midget racer that competed from 1931 until 1954, perhaps the longest, most successful career in air-racing history. The centerpiece of the gallery is the sleek **Hughes H-1** racer, flown by Howard Hughes to a world speed record in 1935 and a transcontinental U.S. speed record in 1937. The H-1 incorporated many advanced design features to minimize drag, including a close-fitting engine cowling; a streamlined, enclosed cockpit; ultrasmooth skin with flush rivets; and retractable landing gear so perfectly fitted that it virtually disappeared into the undersides of the wings.

Throughout the 1920s, aviation remained largely a pursuit for the wealthy. But as technical improvements and a growing market brought the cost of airplanes down, more people began to fly them. They adapted airplanes to a broad range of uses: crop dusting, aerial surveying, transporting cargo and people. Business flying got its start in the Golden Age. The handsome **Beech C17L Staggerwing** that hangs here was fast, comfortable, and expressly designed for business travelers.

The military potential of aircraft was apparent by the end of World War I. The Golden Age saw efforts within the U.S. Army to create an independent air force, promote strategic bombing, and build a heavy bomber. The Navy found ways to adapt aircraft to its own special needs, including taking aviation to sea. Many military aircraft that would see action in World War II emerged in the 1930s. Models and photographs illustrate these developments.

Meanwhile, record-setting flights captured public attention: the first transatlantic flight in 1919 and the first solo crossing in 1927, the first nonstop transcontinental U.S. flight in 1923, the first round-the-world flight in 1924, the first transpacific flight in 1928, the first solo round-the-world flight in 1933. Aviators sought to go ever higher, faster,

Above: The Beech Staggerwing was built for business travel, but Staggerwings also set speed records and won many races.

Below: The 1930s were the golden age of air racing. The Bendix Trophy was awarded to the winner of a transcontinental race first held in 1931.

In this Curtiss Robin, named *Ole Miss*, Fred and Algene Key stayed aloft for 27 days straight. A catwalk built along the front of the fuselage enabled them to service the engine in flight.

farther, and—in the case of the Curtiss J-1 Robin Ole Miss—longer. In 1935 brothers Fred and Algene Key stayed aloft in *Ole Miss* for 27 days, a feat made possible by 432 midair transfers of fuel and supplies.

Uncharted regions of the world beckoned aviators: Africa, the Amazon, the Yucatan, Alaska. Charles and Anne Lindbergh performed aerial archaeological surveys in the American Southwest. Others explored the remote polar regions. On display is the **Northrop Gamma 2B Polar Star,** in which explorer Lincoln Ellsworth and pilot Herbert Hollick-Kenyon set out to traverse Antarctica in 1935. Although they fell slightly short when low fuel forced them down, they became the first to visit the western part of the continent.

Aviation technology made great leaps during the Golden Age, and many modern airplane features emerged. Strut-and-wire–braced wings gave way to single unbraced wings. Metal fuselages replaced wood and fabric. Cockpits became enclosed and landing gear retractable. Better engines were introduced. Displayed here is a water-cooled Curtiss OX-5 engine, vast numbers of which were sold as surplus after World War I. Bought at bargain prices, they helped drive an airplane-building boom in the 1920s. Beside the OX-5 is one of its successors, the powerful, air-cooled Wright Cyclone R-1820-E. Economical, reliable, and easy to

Equipped with skis in place of wheels, the Northrop Gamma Polar Star was flown across Antarctica in 1935. The fuselage area just behind the engine cowling still bears dents from a hard landing on the polar ice.

maintain, the Cyclone became
standard on Navy airplanes
and many commercial airliners.
Oxygen masks, an altimeter, and
a supercharger illustrate how the problems
of high-altitude flight were overcome. At a
nearby video monitor, you can choose among
several short videos to learn more about key
technological advances.

Midway through the gallery, displayed around a screen showing
film clips from the '20s and '30s, are more front pages from several
newspapers. One proclaims in bold type, "Germany Invades Poland"
—three momentous words that signaled the end of aviation's
exuberant Golden Age.

Small treasures and other attractions:

Two films shown in the gallery theater give a good introduction to the
Golden Age: *Jimmy Doolittle Remembers* preserves the firsthand
impressions of one of the era's most famous fliers, and *Benefactors to
Flight* covers the Guggenheim Foundation's contributions to aviation.

Above: Flown by Howard Hughes,
the H-1 was designed to be the
world's fastest landplane. No detail
was overlooked in the effort to make
it as sleek as possible.

Below: The midget racer
Chief Oshkosh, later renamed
Buster. Built by Steve Wittman, this
airplane set records and won many
trophies during its 23-year career.

Pioneers *of* Flight

The 1920s and 1930s were formative decades in aviation on many levels. Flight technology rapidly advanced, military and civilian aviation grew tremendously, record-setting and racing captured headlines and public interest, and African Americans began to breach the social barriers of flight. The interwar period also witnessed the birth of modern rocketry.

The *Barron Hilton Pioneers of Flight Gallery* highlights this exciting era with an eclectic collection of aircraft and other objects. A common theme unites them. All are connected with people who pushed the existing technological or social limits of flight during the early decades of the 20th century. Each aircraft or exhibit represents an unprecedented feat, a barrier overcome, a pioneering step.

The earliest is the **Wright EX *Vin Fiz*** (named after a grape-flavored soft drink sold by the flight's sponsor), in which Calbraith Perry Rodgers, in 1911, became the first to fly across the United States. The trip took about a month and half and involved 70 landings and so many crashes and repairs that the airplane was largely rebuilt en route.

Then consider the **Fokker T-2,** whose wide, thick wings nearly span the gallery. In 1923, two U.S. Army Air Service pilots flew it from Long Island to San Diego, the first nonstop, coast-to-coast flight across the United States. The trip took 27 hours, as Lt. John Macready and Lt. Oakley Kelly navigated with some uncertainty through the night, overcast weather, and rain.

Even after the T-2's successful flight, most people did not consider the airplane a viable or even valuable means of transportation. In 1924 the Army Air Service set out to prove that the airplane was both, by undertaking the first flight around the world. Beneath the T-2's wing is the **Douglas World Cruiser *Chicago,*** one of four airplanes that undertook that mission. Besides being a daring aeronautical venture, the flight required unprecedented logistical and diplomatic effort. Support teams, supplies, and spare parts had to be dispersed to bases around the world. Permission had to be secured for passage through

more than two dozen countries during a time of widespread
international tension and unrest. The two-man crew on each airplane
had no radio or navigational aids and faced climatic conditions ranging
from arctic to tropical. One airplane crashed into a mountainside;
another was lost at sea. But 175 days after leaving Seattle, the *Chicago*
and *New Orleans* returned, having circled the globe.

Throughout the period, record flights and air races captivated the
public. Among the most prestigious races were the Pulitzer Trophy
Race for landplanes and the Schneider Cup Race for seaplanes. The
Curtiss R3C displayed here won both. Flying this plane, Lt. Cyrus Bettis
won the Pulitzer Trophy in 1925. Two weeks later, with streamlined
floats fitted to the R3C, Lt. Jimmy Doolittle won the Schneider Cup,
then set a straight-course world speed record in the same airplane
the very next day.

In the **Lockheed 8 Sirius** *Tingmissartoq*, Charles and Anne Morrow
Lindbergh twice flew across the globe. They first embarked in 1931 on a
vacation flight with "no start or finish, no diplomatic or commercial
significance, and no records to be sought." They did, however, prove

In 1923 the Fokker T-2 became the
first airplane to fly nonstop across
the United States. Two pilots took
turns flying the airplane. One sat in
the open-air cockpit just behind the
engine, while the other awaited his
turn in the cabin below the wing.

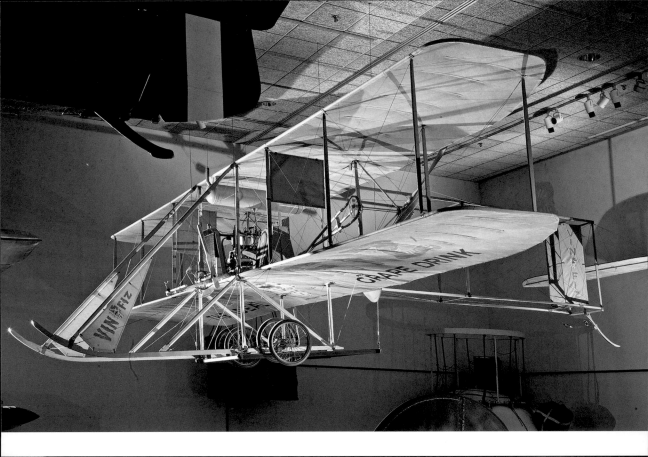

the feasibility of a great circle route from the United States to Asia by flying from Maine to Japan and China via Canada, Alaska, and Siberia. In 1933 they surveyed potential airline routes across the North Atlantic for Pan American Airways, flying from Newfoundland to Europe, down to Africa, across the South Atlantic to South America, and back to the United States.

The bright red **Lockheed 5B Vega** belonged to another renowned aviator, Amelia Earhart. In 1932 she flew it from Newfoundland to Northern Ireland to become the first woman to fly alone nonstop across the Atlantic. A few months later she flew the Vega from Los Angeles to Newark, New Jersey, to become the first woman to fly nonstop across the United States.

The **Piper J-3 Cub** is one of general aviation's greatest success stories, and an example of one hangs here. First built in 1938, J-3s earned fame as a trainers and sport planes. Thousands of pilots over many decades learned to fly in them. Their success made the name "Cub" a generic term for light airplanes.

The *Explorer II* balloon gondola carried Capt. Albert Stevens and Capt. Orvil Anderson to a world record altitude of nearly 72,400 feet in 1935. They performed research in the upper atmosphere and took spectacular photographs, including the first to show the Earth's curvature. Beside the spherical metal gondola is the open-air balloon basket that in 1927 carried Capt. Hawthorne Gray to nearly 42,500 feet, a record flight that cost him his life when he fell unconscious from lack of oxygen.

Modern rocketry began to emerge during this period as well. Robert H. Goddard designed and flew the world's first liquid-fuel rocket in 1926. Displayed here is his **Hoopskirt rocket**—so named because it resembled an old-fashioned hoopskirt. It wasn't meant to be streamlined, but rather to be as light as possible and to test a new operating system. It flew in 1928, the third flight of a liquid-fuel rocket.

Another pioneering achievement represented in this gallery was the decades-long effort by African Americans to break through aviation's racial barriers. "Black Wings" tells that story, highlighting in

Launched in 1935 near Rapid City, South Dakota, the *Explorer II* balloon gondola carried two U.S. Army Air Corps officers to a world record altitude of nearly 72,400 feet.

Opposite Above: In the Wright EX *Vin Fiz*, Calbraith Perry Rodgers in 1911 became the first person to fly across the United States. The trip took about a month and half and involved so many crashes and repairs that the airplane was largely rebuilt en route.

Opposite Below: In 1932 Amelia Earhart flew this Lockheed 5B Vega solo across the Atlantic (the first pilot since Charles Lindbergh to do so) and nonstop across the United States—both firsts for a woman.

Above: Charles and Anne Morrow Lindbergh twice flew this Lockheed 8 Sirius across the globe. At a stop in Greenland on their second trip, an Eskimo boy gave the airplane its name, *Tingmissartoq*—"one who flies like a big bird."

Right: Two Frenchmen in 1783 made the first free flight in human history in the Montgolfier hot-air balloon. Their flight lasted 25 minutes. This is a quarter-scale model of that craft.

Opposite Above: This Curtiss R3C won two prestigious races in 1925: the Pulitzer Trophy Race for landplanes and (fitted with floats) the Schneider Cup Race for seaplanes. Then Jimmy Doolittle flew it to a straight-course world speed record.

Opposite Below: The Douglas World Cruiser *Chicago* was one of two airplanes (of the four that started out on the journey) to complete the first round-the-world flight in 1924.

particular six key people: Bessie Coleman, William J. Powell Jr., James Herman Banning, Cornelius Coffey, Noel F. Parrish, and Benjamin O. Davis Jr. The latter two were involved with the famed Tuskegee Airmen of World War II.

Small treasures and other attractions:

Hanging in one corner is a quarter-scale model of the colorful Montgolfier hot-air balloon, in which two Frenchmen in 1783 made the first free flight in human history. In the other corner is the *Bud Light Spirit of Freedom* balloon gondola, in which Steve Fossett in 2002 became the first person to fly solo around the world by balloon. An enclosed area where young children can enjoy themselves in an aviation-theme environment occupies part of the gallery.

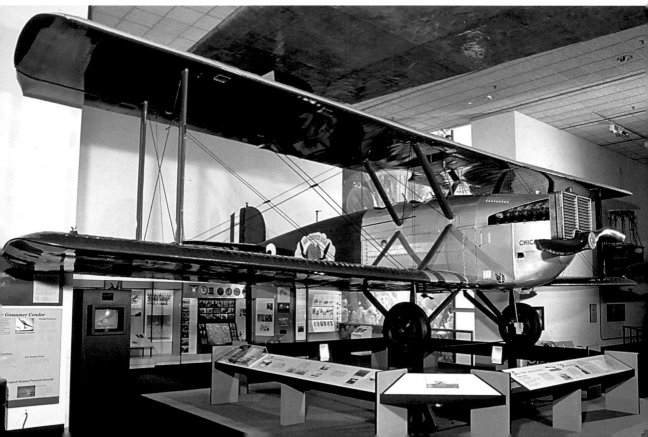

World War II Aviation

Upon entering this gallery, you suddenly find yourself almost nose to nose with the B-17 Flying Fortress *Thunder Bird* roaring out of a clear blue sky over Wiesbaden, Germany, contrails streaming behind it, German fighters angling in from four and seven o'clock. You can make out the faces of the aircrew in the cockpit and nose of the bomber. You can count the bombs—71, each representing a mission—painted on its fuselage. The mural, *Fortresses Under Fire* by Keith Ferris, fills the entire rear wall and can be seen throughout the gallery. It freezes a single, furious moment in history's biggest and most destructive war.

Like an actual B-17 bomber, the full story of aviation's role in World War II is too big to present in this gallery. Instead, *World War II Aviation* concentrates on land-based fighter aviation, as epitomized by the five fighter airplanes on display. Also here are examples of significant engines; bombs, armament, and ammunition; and aircrew and service uniforms from many nations.

Bomber aircraft are represented by the forward fuselage of the **B-26 Marauder** *Flak Bait*. With 202 bombs hand-painted on its side, this two-engine medium bomber flew more missions over Europe than any other Allied aircraft, including two missions on D-Day. Its name proved apt. Shrapnel and bullets riddled *Flak Bait* with more than a thousand holes—you can see some of the riveted patches— and several times nearly crippled the plane. You can look into the nose, where the bombardier sat at his Norden bombsight, and into the area just behind the cockpit for a sense of what the inside of a bomber is like. Nearby, combat film footage from the 1944 documentary *Memphis Belle* vividly shows what flying daylight missions over Europe was like for bomber crews.

The gallery features beautifully restored fighter airplanes from five nations. Royal Air Force pilots flying the legendary **Supermarine Spitfire** defended Great Britain against German bomber attacks to help win the crucial Battle of Britain. More than 20,000 Spitfires were built,

and they fought on every major battlefront. The airplane displayed here, a Mark VII high-altitude model, never saw combat; it went straight from the factory to the U.S. Army Air Forces for evaluation. Beside it is a Rolls-Royce Merlin engine, which powered the Spitfire and other British fighters and bombers.

One of the adversaries those British pilots faced was the **Messerschmitt Bf 109.** The 109 became widely known and feared during Germany's blitzkrieg (lightning war) against Poland and other countries. Allied bombers over Europe faced relentless swarms of 109s throughout the war. This Bf 109G-6 was captured when its pilot, a Frenchman flying for the Germans, defected in Italy in 1944. Beside the airplane is a Daimler-Benz DB 605 engine, one in the series that powered Bf 109s.

Though less well-known than the Bf 109, the Italian **Macchi C.202 Folgore** (Lightning) was an effective fighter that could outmaneuver and outperform most of its adversaries. Folgores were flown by Italian and German pilots against the Allies in North Africa and elsewhere,

Above: Japan produced more Mitsubishi Zeros than any other warplane. Zeros fought throughout the Pacific in nearly every major battle involving the Japanese navy. This one was probably captured on Saipan.

Below: Riddled with more than 1,000 holes from shells and shrapnel, *Flak Bait* earned its name. Still, the tough old bird completed a record 202 bombing missions over Europe.

Inside *Flak Bait*, one of only a few surviving B-26 Marauders.

First unveiled at the 1936 Olympic Games in Berlin, the Messerschmitt Bf 109 remained one of Germany's principal fighters throughout World War II. Its armament included a cannon that fired through the propeller hub.

Opposite Above: The Supermarine Spitfire was a mainstay of Britain's fighter defense during World War II. It has a distinctive elliptical wing shape, which reduced drag and increased the airplane's speed.

Opposite Below: *World War II Aviation* features airplanes from five nations, including this North American P-51D Mustang. One of the finest fighters of the war, the P-51 had the range to escort high-altitude Allied bombers deep into Europe.

and later by Italian pilots against Germany. About 1,200 were produced, more than any other Italian monoplane fighter. The Folgore displayed here is one of only two that still exist.

The best fighters possessed a winning combination of superior speed, range, maneuverability, and firepower. One of the finest fighters of World War II, the **North American P-51D Mustang** had all these attributes. It was the first fighter with enough range to escort Allied bombers deep into Europe and was a terror at strafing as well. North American developed the Mustang in 1940 for the British, who were in desperate need of fighters. The powerful Rolls-Royce Merlin engine, used on the British Spitfire, was later incorporated into the Mustang, greatly increasing its performance. Mustangs saw action in every major theater. The P-51 displayed here never left the United States; it was used for training by the Air National Guard.

Among the first enemy aircraft Americans faced was the **Mitsubishi A6M Zero.** The Japanese navy's main fighter, the Zero was used in the attack on Pearl Harbor and throughout the Pacific theater, including kamikaze attacks late in the war. Fast and maneuverable and with excellent range, Zeros seemed to rule the sky in the early months of the war. But Allied pilots learned to capitalize on their own superior

firepower and diving speed, and the
introduction of the new Hellcats and Mustangs
decisively ended the Zero's reign.

The Zero is best seen from the gallery's mezzanine, which also
provides a closer view of two concept paintings created by Robert T.
McCall for the film *Tora! Tora! Tora!,* a 1970 Hollywood production
about the Japanese attack on Pearl Harbor. Also on the mezzanine are
exhibits on airplane recognition models, ammunition, the 1942

Doolittle raid on Japan, battle damage to airplanes, aces, Army Air Forces Gen. Henry "Hap" Arnold, the WASPs and other women pilots, and uniforms and flying gear.

Small treasures and other attractions:

One exhibit case is devoted to the famous Flying Tigers, the American volunteer fighter group that operated out of China. Another case contains medals, flight gear, and other items that belonged to pilots of the all-black 332nd Fighter Group of the famous Tuskegee Airmen. Yet another is crammed with personal mementos of other men and women who served: snapshots that capture moments of rest and relaxation between missions, photos of Betty Grable and other pinup girls, a magazine centerfold, a Bill Mauldin cartoon, a membership card for a dance club and an eight-hour pass, a box of K rations and a pack of Chesterfields, a souvenir piece of shrapnel, a pocket-size New Testament, a scrap of paper noting that "Kilroy was here."

The Keith Ferris mural *Fortresses Under Fire* fills an entire wall of the gallery.

Opposite: This Italian Macchi Folgore made up for its inferior armament with its performance and maneuverability. Its left wing is slightly longer than its right— an unusual feature designed to help counteract engine torque.

Sea-Air Operations

No other gallery transports you to another environment quite like *Sea-Air Operations*. You don't enter: you come aboard. The shrill whistle of a bosun's call sounds as you cross onto the quarterdeck (the boarding and ceremonial area) of the mythical aircraft carrier USS *Smithsonian*. Inside is a scaled-down re-creation of a bay on a hangar deck, the area below the flight deck where aircraft maintenance and repair work take place. The surrounding structures and equipment are from an actual aircraft carrier. The "views" are projections of films taken on a carrier at sea.

Beyond the hangar bay, you can also poke around in a ready room, a combined living room and briefing area for a squadron flight crew. Or you can go upstairs and visit the navigation bridge and PriFly (Primary Flight Control), the air traffic control center for this seaborne airfield. From these two rooms you can watch "cat shots" and "traps" (takeoffs and landings) filmed on the USS *Enterprise*. Balconies overlook the hangar bay and four vintage airplanes that span a half century of carrier aviation.

The **Boeing F4B-4** biplane was the last in a series of aircraft that served as the main fighter for the U.S. Navy and Army Air Corps from the late 1920s to the mid-1930s. This airplane was built for the Marine Corps. Of the hundreds of F4Bs produced, only one, an airplane sold to China that engaged the Japanese, ever saw combat.

The **Grumman F4F Wildcat** saw plenty of combat, at Wake Island, the Coral Sea, Midway, and Guadalcanal. Designed in the 1930s, Wildcats were the Navy's most widely used carrier-based fighter during the early months of World War II. Although Wildcats could not match the maneuverability of the Japanese Zero and were often outnumbered, the skill and teamwork of their pilots and the aircraft's heavy armament helped compensate. These tough fighters helped prevent the Japanese from dominating the skies until better fighters could enter combat. This airplane, which served as a trainer, is an FM-1, a version manufactured by the Eastern Aircraft Division of General Motors. Its

front cowling, from an airplane that saw combat at Wake Island, was formerly part of the Wake Island Memorial, which was dedicated to those who fought in that battle.

The **Douglas SBD-6 Dauntless** was the Navy's standard dive-bomber when the United States entered the war. Design changes based on combat experience, including additional armor, a more powerful engine, and better armament, made the aircraft increasingly effective. While SBD stood for "Scout Bomber Douglas," pilots dubbed the Dauntless "Slow But Deadly." It proved that reputation at the Battle of the Coral Sea and at Midway, where SBDs sank four Japanese carriers and helped turn the tide of war.

Representing post–World War II carrier aircraft is the **Douglas A-4C Skyhawk**, a versatile attack-bomber designed in the early 1950s and used by the Navy and Marine Corps throughout the Vietnam War. Lightweight and compact—its short wings do not fold for storage like most carrier aircraft—it could nonetheless carry a large allotment of bombs, rockets, and machine guns. Skyhawks provided close support for ground troops and attacked other ground targets with notable accuracy. The Skyhawk on display served on the USS *Bon Homme Richard* and took part in combat operations against North Vietnam

The Douglas SBD Dauntless dive-bomber helped turn the tide of World War II in the Pacific. The airplane carried a large bomb beneath its fuselage and smaller bombs on its wings.

BOMB ELEV
A-109-T

FIRE PLUG
1-62-1-1-6

from March to June 1967. It bears the name of Cmdr. Robert Byron Fuller, to whom the airplane was assigned at the time. Fuller was later shot down over North Vietnam and remained a prisoner until the war's end.

Sea-Air Operations contains two other exhibits. "Carrier Warfare in the Pacific" traces the early development of the aircraft carrier and focuses on the six carrier-versus-carrier battles of World War II. The first four battles took place in 1942: Coral Sea was the first sea battle fought by air alone; Midway, a month later, marked the turning point of the Pacific war; the battles in the Eastern Solomons and the Santa Cruz Islands were fought over control of Guadalcanal. The two other battles occurred in 1944: the Battle of the Philippine Sea, during the Allied invasion of the Marianas; and the Battle of Leyte Gulf, the largest sea battle in history, during the invasion of the Philippines. These stories are told through photographs, Movietone Newsreel footage, aircraft models, flight suits, and other artifacts.

The second exhibit, "Modern Carrier Aviation," picks up where "Carrier Warfare" leaves off. It traces aircraft carrier development since World War II and focuses on carrier operations today. Displays here examine life on board a carrier, landing an airplane, catapults and

The Douglas A-4C Skyhawk attack-bomber saw extensive use during the Vietnam War. This Skyhawk flew combat missions over North Vietnam in 1967 from the aircraft carrier *Bon Homme Richard*.

Opposite Above: The Grumman Wildcat was the U.S. Navy's main carrier fighter for the first two years of World War II. This version has a mechanism that allows the wings to fold back against the fuselage.

Opposite Below: The Boeing F4B-4 served as the main fighter for the U.S. Navy from the late 1920s to the mid-1930s. This F4B-4 was built for the Marine Corps.

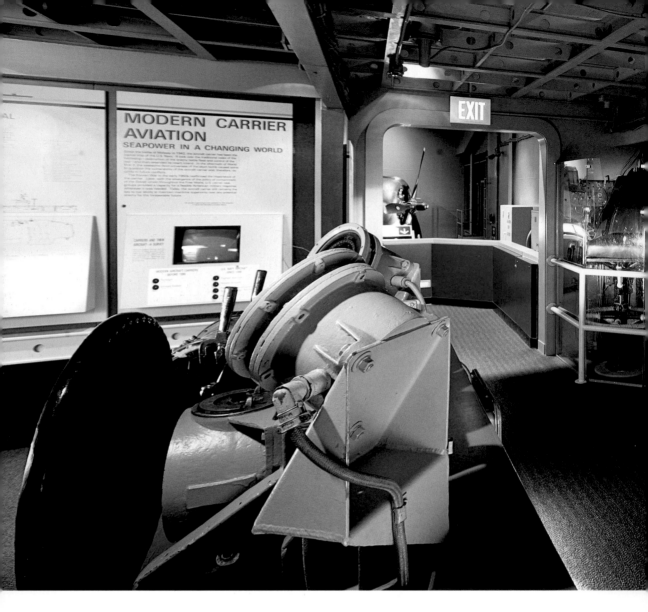

The gallery's re-created navigation bridge, which provides an unobstructed view of a carrier's flight deck and the surrounding air and sea.

arresting gear, carrier aircraft, weapons, the use of naval forces during the Cold War and afterward, and the building of the USS *Enterprise,* the first nuclear-powered carrier. Exhibits include aircraft models, a section of an arresting gear cable, air-to-air missiles from an F-14 Tomcat, and a model of the optical landing system used on modern carriers.

Seaborne aviation has come a long way since Eugene Ely took off in a Curtiss biplane from a wooden platform built on the bow of a Navy cruiser in 1910, then reversed the feat two months later by landing on another cruiser. The carrier is now the "capital ship" of the Navy, and one of the most complex weapon systems in the world.

Small treasures and other attractions:

You can examine the propeller from the biplane that made the first
flight off a ship in 1910, then try to guide an F/A-18 Hornet to a landing
on a modern carrier deck using a computer flight simulator in the
hangar bay. Also on display is Tom W. Freeman's painting *Too Close
for Comfort*, which depicts Lt. j.g. Donald D. Engen, the Museum's late
director, flying his Helldiver against the Japanese fleet during the Battle
of Leyte Gulf. And don't miss the 1/100th-scale model of the nuclear-
powered USS *Enterprise*, exquisitely detailed right down to the sprinkler
pipes on the ceilings of the hangar bays and the fuel hoses and reels
along the deck.

Jet Aviation

In 1939, at the trailing edge of the Golden Age of Flight, an experimental airplane with a new kind of engine lifted off from an airfield in Germany. The brainchild of a young German engineer named Hans von Ohain, the propellerless turbojet engine used hot, high-speed exhaust gases to produce thrust and was amazingly powerful for its weight. Across the continent, a young English engineer named Frank Whittle had developed a remarkably similar power plant based on the same principle. His engine would fly in 1941. While they created their engines concurrently, at the time neither man knew of the other's work.

As the world became immersed in war, new aircraft were produced by the thousands, with improved designs rolling out one after another. Then in mid-1944, a radical new German airplane appeared in the skies. Pilots who witnessed the propellerless, turbojet-powered Me 262 fighter scream past them must have thought they'd seen something out of the future. But they hadn't—the jet age had already begun.

Since then turbojet engines have transformed military and commercial aviation. They have made possible aircraft that can fly farther, faster, and higher and that are larger and more efficient than piston-engine aircraft. Propeller-driven aircraft are still widely used, but jets now dominate most types of aviation. *Jet Aviation* traces the development of this technology and features many important turbojet engines introduced over four decades, along with three airplanes that helped usher in the jet age.

Exhibits near the entrance explain the principles of jet propulsion and jet aircraft design. Animated diagrams show how a turbine engine works and compare the three main types: turbojet, turbofan, and turboprop. Nearby, an automated model demonstrates the various moving parts of a Lockheed L-1011 jetliner wing. Cases filled with scale-model jets and photos document the early milestones of jet aviation. Above, wings folded, is a **McDonnell FH-1 Phantom**, which served with Marine Fighter Squadron 122. In 1946 a prototype

MILITARY JET PILOT'S EQUIPMENT

The Lockheed XP-80 *Lulu Belle* was the prototype for the first U.S. jet fighter to enter full production. In contrast to the German Me 262, it has straight rather than swept wings, and its single jet engine is embedded in its fuselage.

Opposite: The world's first operational jet fighter, the Messerschmitt Me 262 outperformed the best Allied fighters of World War II. But it entered combat too late to have much impact on the war.

Overleaf: The Pratt & Whitney JT9D was the first of the very large, high-bypass turbofan engines to enter commercial service. It powered the Boeing 747 on its first flight in 1969.

Phantom became the first U.S. jet to take off and land on an aircraft carrier. Soon thereafter, the Phantom became the first jet fighter of the Navy and Marine Corps, the harbinger of a new era in naval aviation.

A huge mural by Keith Ferris, *The Evolution of Jet Aviation,* spans the center of the gallery. It depicts 27 jet aircraft, from the first jet, the Heinkel He 178, to the fastest, the Lockheed SR-71 Blackbird. In front of the mural are the two milestone engines developed by von Ohain and Whittle, the co-creators of the turbojet engine. Von Ohain's Heinkel HeS 3B is a cutaway reproduction that reveals the engine's internal details. Whittle's W1X is the type that powered the Gloster E. 28/39, the first British jet to become airborne. A film segment from a BBC program on the British turbojet effort includes accounts from surprised bystanders, astonished to see a propellerless airplane whistling by. A video display allows you to select film clips of 92 jet aircraft, including rare footage from some of the earliest jets.

Others engines include a cutaway model of the Pratt & Whitney JT3/J57, an engine of unprecedented power used on such diverse aircraft as the North American F-100 fighter, the Boeing B-52 bomber, and the Boeing 707 jetliner; a General Electric CJ805/J79, which powered the Lockheed F-104 Starfighter and McDonnell Douglas F-4

Phantom II fighters; and the Lycoming T53, a turboprop/turboshaft engine adapted to such helicopters as the Bell UH-1 Iroquois.

The gallery's twin centerpieces are two jet-age milestones. The German **Messerschmitt Me 262**, the airplane that so surprised Allied pilots, became the first jet fighter in the world to enter operational service when unleashed in 1944. Lean and sharklike in appearance,

with its distinctive flattened fuselage, pointed nose, and swept-back wings, the Me 262 could outperform any Allied fighter. It could outfly the formidable P-51 Mustang by 120 miles per hour, and its four nose-mounted cannons could tear a bomber to pieces. The Me 262 offered Germany its best hope for regaining control of its own skies. When its aircraft factories and airfields were bombed into ruins, Germany resorted to building the jets in forest clearings and launching them from its autobahns. The lethal fighter failed to break the Allied dominance of the air, but it radically changed the future of aerial warfare.

The United States got a late start behind Germany and Britain in jet development. The **Lockheed XP-80 Lulu Belle** marked the U.S. drive to catch up. Led by the legendary Clarence "Kelly" Johnson, Lockheed's famous "Skunk Works" designed and constructed the XP-80 in just 143 days. The *Lulu Belle* first flew in January 1944. Its success led to the first full-production, operational jet fighter for the United States, the P-80 Shooting Star, later redesignated the F-80. Shooting Stars entered combat and saw extensive action in the Korean War. In 1950 an F-80 scored the first jet-versus-jet combat victory.

Relocated from the *Pioneers of Flight* gallery is a jet-powered aircraft of a very different type: the **Bell 206 LongRanger II** *Spirit of Texas* helicopter. Pilots H. Ross Perot Jr. and Jay Coburn flew it around the world in 1982, the first time this feat had been accomplished by helicopter.

Small treasures and other attractions:

Dwarfed by the larger engines is the tiny Williams WR19 turbofan, used on such intriguing experimental projects as a jet-powered backpack, a two-person flying platform, and a combination ejection seat–autogiro for a fighter aircraft. The gallery theater presents "Sneaking Through the Sound Barrier," a vintage TV spoof starring Sid Caesar, Imogene Coca, and Carl Reiner.

The Keith Ferris mural *The Evolution of Jet Aviation* fills an entire wall of the gallery. The painting includes 27 significant jet aircraft, from the first to the fastest.

Opposite: A McDonnell FH-1 Phantom rests with wings folded in a corner of the gallery. The Phantom was the first jet to take off and land on an aircraft carrier, and it became the first jet fighter of the U.S. Navy and Marine Corps.

Beyond *the* Limits
FLIGHT ENTERS THE COMPUTER AGE

Consider the chip: that tiny silicon wafer, also known as the integrated circuit, found in everything from talking toys to supercomputers. Ever smaller, ever more powerful, and ever more versatile, chips are the driving force behind the computer revolution. So ubiquitous is the chip, so seamlessly integrated into almost every aspect of our lives, that its impact can hardly be overstated.

Beyond the Limits examines how computers have transformed flight in all its aspects. Small objects on display range from analog calculating devices that preceded computers to instruments and imagery that show where digital technology is headed. Large objects include two experimental aircraft and a communications satellite, each an important aerospace application of computer technology. Interactive computers throughout the gallery invite you to design an airplane or rocket, try out a flight simulation program, manipulate shapes as an aircraft designer would, or find the shortest air route between several cities.

The first electronic computers were essentially huge, electronic calculators that relied on vacuum tubes and were big enough to fill a large room. The transistor, invented in 1947, made computers far smaller and far more powerful. At the gallery entrance, a pillar of transistors juxtaposed with a single tiny chip symbolizes the impact of the integrated circuit; one chip can now perform operations that would have required millions of transistors.

Aviation and spaceflight both benefited from and helped drive the computer revolution. Since war research in the 1940s produced the first electronic computers, aerospace and defense industry needs have spurred innovation. The Minuteman III guidance system on display exemplifies this relationship. Requirements for the Minuteman III guided missile in the 1960s led to the mass manufacturing of chips,

which later led to widespread applications of computer technology in the consumer world.

Aircraft design was one of the first fields transformed by computers. A large teaching version of a slide rule, once an essential tool of every aircraft designer and engineer, and a Friden mechanical calculator from 1953 evoke the laborious nature of aircraft design at a time when drawings were done by hand and when "computers" were people, typically women, who "crunched numbers" on mechanical calculators. The first electronic computers were expensive, cumbersome, and not always reliable, but aerospace companies were among the first to acquire them. Computers proved essential for the complex calculations required by new jet aircraft and rocket designs. Ultimately, computer-aided design (CAD) and computer-aided manufacturing (CAM) would make design and manufacturing far easier, faster, and more precise.

Beginning with the Wright brothers, aircraft designers have relied on scale aircraft models mounted in wind tunnels to test new designs. In the 1970s a machine powerful enough to process complex aerodynamic data was created: the supercomputer. Since then, designers have used computers to supplement and even supplant

The unusual design of the Grumman X-29 fighter, with its forward-swept wings and forward stabilizer, makes the airplane very unstable but very agile. The pilot must rely on three onboard computers to maintain stability.

A network of 66 satellites like this one formed the heart of Iridium, a space-based communications system that for the first time enabled handheld mobile phone users to communicate anywhere in the world.

wind tunnel testing. On display is a Cray-1 supercomputer from 1976, with some of its panels removed to reveal its banks of circuits and miles of wiring. In striking contrast to the comparatively compact Cray is a bulky memory unit from the U.S. Air Force's SAGE computer, which dates from 1959 and used 30,000 vacuum tubes. Hanging overhead is one of the first aircraft designed mostly by computer, the **HiMAT** (Highly Maneuverable Aircraft Technology). Flown from 1979 to 1983, this small-scale test aircraft was developed to help improve combat maneuverability. Unmanned, it was controlled by a pilot on the ground.

While computers and wind tunnels can predict the behavior of an aircraft in flight, actual flight testing remains essential. Computers have made the data gathering and analysis of flight testing easier and more efficient, replacing the strip charts, tape, and film once used to record aircraft performance.

Onboard computers have enhanced aircraft capabilities beyond what was previously possible. On display is a full-scale model of the **Grumman X-29** fighter, which first flew in 1984. This experimental aircraft is so unstable that a pilot cannot fly it without computer assistance, but this instability makes the X-29 exceptionally maneuverable. Computer-aided control also made feasible the "flying wing," a concept pioneered in the 1940s but not perfected until the B-2 Stealth bomber of the 1990s. Models of the Stealth and earlier flying wings are on display.

Computers have transformed other aspects of air and space operations, from air traffic control and airline ticketing, to aircraft and spacecraft guidance systems, to pilot training. Flight simulation once relied on devices such as the quaint Link "Blue Box" Trainer exhibited here. Simulations are now far more realistic and effective, thanks to computer graphic displays and computer-guided feedback systems.

Aerospace computer technology has also made possible space-based, global telecommunications systems and the Global Positioning System (GPS), which allows instant and accurate position determination. The gallery features an exhibit on GPS as well as an **Iridium satellite.** While an economic failure, a network of Iridium satellites in low Earth orbit enabled handheld mobile phone users to communicate anywhere in the world for the first time.

In the "Earth Today" theater, you can check out current conditions on our planet. Data collected by satellites and other global monitoring systems are relayed to the Museum, processed by a supercomputer, and projected onto the screen here.

Small treasures and other attractions:

Among the many vintage instruments on display are the typewriter-size Marchant calculator, which could multiply two numbers in 10 seconds; the American Airlines Reservisor, a pre-Internet keyboard device used for airline ticketing; the tiny model globe used by astronaut John Glenn to plot his position during his 1962 Mercury flight; the Gemini guidance computer, the first onboard digital computer used on a manned spacecraft; and a sky chart and slide rule of the type used by Apollo astronauts to help them navigate to the Moon. An exhibit on flight data and voice recorders displays instruments, including the so-called "black box," used to determine causes of aircraft accidents. At the GPS exhibit, you can set your watch by the time relayed from a GPS satellite—the digital readout is accurate to within 150-billionths of a second.

This Minuteman III missile guidance system illustrates how aerospace and defense industry needs have spurred innovation. Development of the Minuteman III in the 1960s led to the mass manufacturing of chips, which led to their widespread use in many other applications.

Opposite: HiMAT is a 4/10-scale research aircraft that was used to test new concepts in design, construction, and control. It was piloted from the ground by computer-assisted remote control.

Military Unmanned Aerial Vehicles

The U.S. military experimented with unmanned aircraft as early as World War I. During World War II, glide bombs and radio-controlled B-17 drones filled with explosives came into use. In the 1950s, recoverable unmanned vehicles were developed for reconnaissance purposes, and versions armed with weapons soon followed.

Today, Unmanned Aerial Vehicles, or UAVs, perform reconnaissance, surveillance, target acquisition, bomb-damage assessment, and attack missions. Some carry sensors and cameras; others, offensive weapons. Six examples hang in this gallery, ranging from the large and lethal to the tiny and portable.

The **Lockheed Martin/Boeing RQ-3A DarkStar** is a stealthy reconnaissance UAV designed to provide near real-time target data and imagery by way of satellite links to a mobile ground station. The DarkStar never made it to operational use, unlike the **General Atomics MQ-1L Predator.** Predators have performed attack missions over the Balkans, Afghanistan, and Iraq. The one hanging here flew 196 combat missions in Afghanistan.

The stealthy, swept-wing, jet-powered **Boeing X-45A** was the first modern UAV designed specifically for combat strike missions. This X-45A, with two internal weapons bays, is a scaled-down technology demonstrator used for testing. The **Pioneer UAV RQ-2A Pioneer** displayed here has a special distinction. During the 1991 Gulf War, while the unarmed aircraft was assessing damage from naval gunfire, several Iraqi soldiers signaled their intention to surrender to it during a low pass—the first time anyone had ever surrendered to a UAV.

The **AAI Corporation RQ-7A Shadow 200** performs a wide range of non-attack missions. It can take off or land on fixed landing gear or be launched by catapult and land using a tail hook and arresting cables.

The General Atomics MQ-1L Predator hanging here flew nearly 200 combat missions in Afghanistan.

Right: The stealthy Boeing X-45A was the first modern UAV designed specifically for combat strike missions.

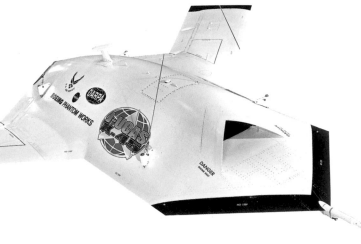

Opposite: The Museum's West Gallery displays several military unmanned aerial vehicles—UAVs—used for reconnaissance, surveillance, target acquisition, bomb damage assessment, and attack.

Overleaf: An aerial view of the Museum's West Gallery.

The **AeroVironment RQ-14A Dragon Eye** is by far the smallest aircraft here. This hand- or bungee-launched mini-UAV can provide reconnaissance and surveillance information to field commanders. A Dragon Eye system consists of three UAVs and their ground control equipment, all of which are light and compact enough to be carried in a Marine's backpack.

SPACE

The *Space Race* gallery.

GALLERIES

Space Race

Soon after World War II, the United States and the Soviet Union became locked in a global conflict pitting democracy against communism. Space became a critical theater in this Cold War, as each side competed to best the other's achievements. Some of this competition took place in public view, some in great secrecy. The launch of Sputnik 1 in 1957 marked the first great victory in what came to be known as the Space Race. A dozen years later, the race decisively ended on a dusty plain of the Moon.

The breakup of the Soviet Union and the end of the Cold War presented the National Air and Space Museum with an unexpected opportunity. In Russia, historic space artifacts were being made available to collectors. In the United States, objects from once top-secret programs were being declassified. The time was ripe for mounting a major exhibition on the U.S.-Soviet competition in space.

Space Race tells about the U.S.-Soviet space rivalry and its aftermath, from the military origins of the Space Race, through the race to the Moon and the development of reconnaissance satellites, to cooperative ventures between the two former rivals and efforts to maintain a human presence in space. Rockets, spacecraft, and many other artifacts documenting U.S. space endeavors are juxtaposed with rare and historic examples of Soviet space technology.

The first of four major sections, "Military Origins of the Space Race" examines the developments in rocketry that made the Space Race possible. The German **V-2 missile** was the first ballistic missile used to strike distant targets. Nearly 3,000 were launched against England, France, and Belgium during World War II, killing thousands of people. An ominous harbinger of a new kind of warfare, the V-2 sparked large-scale rocketry efforts in both the United States and the Soviet Union.

A cluster of rockets illustrates the roles these vehicles played in the Space Race. The U.S. Army's **WAC Corporal**, a high-altitude test rocket, represents the state of American rocketry at the end of World War II. The U.S. Navy's **Viking** was used to launch scientific

instruments into the upper atmosphere. The **Jupiter-C** boosted the first U.S. satellite, **Explorer 1**, into orbit in 1958, while the Vanguard rocket delivered the second. The **Aerobee 150** exemplifies a family of rockets used from the 1940s to the 1980s for atmospheric research. The **Scout-D** launched scientific satellites from the 1960s to the 1990s. The **Minuteman III** intercontinental ballistic missile has been a U.S. strategic weapon since 1970. Nearby hang two weapons that span the history of cruise missiles: the **V-1**, sometimes called a "buzz bomb," which was used by Germany during World War II; and a **Tomahawk** cruise missile, used by the U.S. Navy since 1982.

"Racing to the Moon" examines the most prominent aspect of the Space Race. Stunned by the Soviet Union's 1957 launching of Sputnik, the first artificial satellite, the United States scrambled to catch up. The damaged **Vanguard** satellite on display was recovered from one of two failed U.S. attempts to launch a satellite. Explorer 1 achieved orbit in 1958, but the Soviets stayed a step ahead. On display is one of the earliest "space travelers" to orbit the Earth—a Soviet flight-test mannequin named Ivan Ivanovich. The first human in space, cosmonaut Yuri Gagarin, circled the Earth a few weeks later in April 1961. The Soviet Union also launched the first spacecraft to the Moon,

During the Apollo-Soyuz Test Project in 1975, U.S. and Soviet spacecraft docked in space. Here, the command and service modules of an Apollo spacecraft are linked by a docking module to a Soyuz spacecraft. The Apollo is a test vehicle, the Soyuz a full-scale model.

Overleaf: *Space Race* contains a wealth of artifacts from both the U.S. and Soviet space programs.

sent the first woman into space, and carried out the first "spacewalk." You can examine the spacecraft airlock attachment and Berkut pressure suit used in training by Aleksei Leonov, the first man to walk in space.

President John F. Kennedy's declaration in 1961 that the United States would land a man on the Moon focused the Space Race on that goal. Spacesuits help illustrate the story of how the United States surpassed the Soviet Union in the race to the Moon. Yuri Gagarin's SK-1 pressure suit, worn during training for his historic flight, is juxtaposed with John Glenn's spacesuit, which he wore in

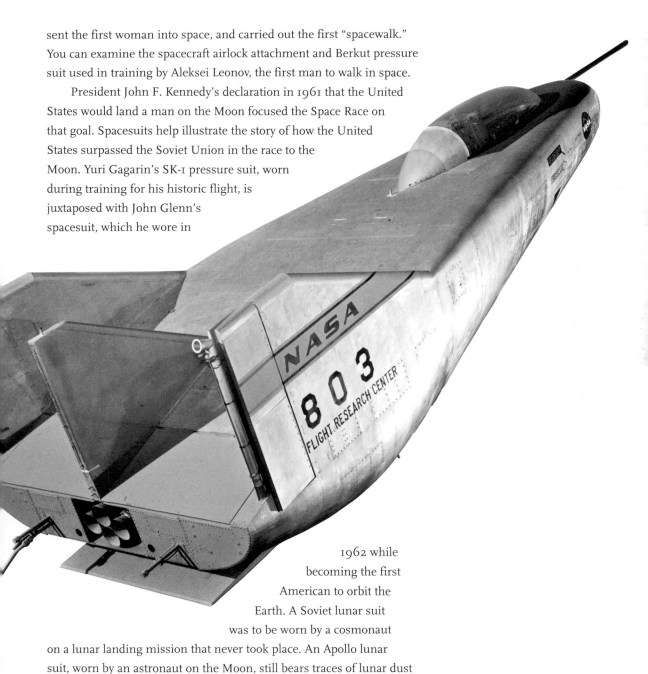

1962 while becoming the first American to orbit the Earth. A Soviet lunar suit was to be worn by a cosmonaut on a lunar landing mission that never took place. An Apollo lunar suit, worn by an astronaut on the Moon, still bears traces of lunar dust on the legs and boots.

"Satellite Reconnaissance: Secret Eyes in Space" relates an aspect of the Space Race long concealed from the public. Within months after the launch of Sputnik, worries about the possibility of a surprise nuclear attack by the Soviet Union prompted President Dwight D.

Test vehicles such as this M2-F3 lifting body—a wingless aircraft that derives lift from its shape—were a crucial step in developing the Space Shuttle orbiter.

GLENN'S SPACE SUIT

GAGARIN'S SPACE SUIT

Eisenhower to authorize a secret, top-priority project, code-named Corona, to develop reconnaissance satellites. Corona satellites could take high-resolution photos of the Soviet Union and return the film to Earth for analysis.

Declassified in 1995, the Corona camera exhibited here could resolve objects as small as about six feet across. Beside it is a Corona film-return capsule, designed to be jettisoned from the satellite and snagged in midair by a recovery aircraft as the capsule parachuted to Earth. A Salyut film-return capsule from a similar Soviet system is also on display, along with a Soviet **Merkur** manned spacecraft, which was launched as part of an experimental military space station module in 1983.

"A Permanent Presence in Space" became the focus of the U.S. and Soviet manned spaceflight programs after the Moon race ended. The **Skylab Orbital Workshop** was a backup component for the first U.S. space station, which astronaut crews occupied for nearly six months in 1973–74. The **Apollo-Soyuz Test Project**, during which U.S. and Soviet craft docked in space in 1975, marked the first cooperative mission by the two rivals. The Apollo spacecraft here is a test vehicle; the Soyuz is a full-scale model.

Yuri Gagarin wore this orange pressure suit during training for his 1961 flight, when he became the first man in space. John Glenn wore the silver spacesuit during his 1962 flight, when he became the first American to orbit the Earth.

Opposite: The German V-2 was the first ballistic missile used to strike distant targets. After World War II, both the United States and the Soviet Union used captured V-2s to help them develop their own large rockets.

The Soviet Union concentrated on developing space stations designed for continuous habitation. The **Soyuz TM-10** spacecraft returned two cosmonauts and a Japanese journalist to Earth from the space station Mir. The United States developed the reusable Space Shuttle to ferry astronauts into space and back on short but frequent missions. One of the early test vehicles that contributed to the shuttle's design was the **M2-F3 lifting body**, a wingless aircraft that derived lift from its fuselage shape. NASA built and flew the craft during the 1960s. On one Space Shuttle mission, astronauts placed in orbit the **Hubble Space Telescope**; a full-size test version stands in the gallery. Spacesuits and clothing on display—such as those of Guion Bluford, the first African American in space, and Sally Ride, the first American woman in space—testify to the diversity of the current astronaut corps. An exhibit on the International Space Station highlights our most ambitious effort yet to maintain an ongoing presence in space.

Photos taken by Corona spy satellites were returned to Earth in nose-cone capsules like this one. More advanced reconnaissance satellites—still classified—have since replaced Corona.

Opposite: Placed in orbit by Space Shuttle astronauts in 1990, the Hubble Space Telescope has been one of the great success stories of space-based astronomy.

Small treasures and other attractions:

The tiny metal arming key used on Sputnik I prior to its launch is the only remaining piece of the satellite that ushered in the space age. Also here are objects used by a Minuteman missileer, including the bag that contained his launch instructions and a deck of cards used to while away the long duty hours. Poignant reminders of space exploration's human toll include plaques commemorating the *Challenger* and *Columbia* Space Shuttle crews. You can learn the answer to that delicate question, "How do astronauts go to the bathroom in space?" and examine "human waste disposal units" from Soyuz and Mir. And don't miss the display of stunning images from the Hubble Space Telescope.

Above: Inside the Skylab orbital workshop, which you can enter.

Right: The Soviets developed this spacesuit for cosmonauts to wear on the Moon.

Opposite: America's first space station, Skylab was launched into orbit in 1973. This large cylinder with attached solar panels is the backup Skylab orbital workshop, the space station's largest component.

Apollo *to the* Moon

The titanic scale and complexity of the Apollo program reflected the boldness of the U.S. commitment to send men to the Moon. When President Kennedy set the nation on that course in 1961, America had been trailing the Soviet Union in the Space Race for more than three years and had sent only one astronaut, Alan Shepard, into space on a brief suborbital flight. By the time the program ended, it had employed the efforts of more than a half-million people, produced the largest and most powerful rockets ever built, and sent humans farther than they had ever gone before.

The great achievements of the Apollo program rested upon many small ones, upon thousands of technical innovations and boundless ingenuity. The heart of *Apollo to the Moon* is its unparalleled display of artifacts from Apollo and earlier missions that bring this sweeping endeavor down to a human scale. The items range from the critical (fuel cells to produce electricity) to the mundane (a tube of pureed beef stew carried by John Glenn on *Friendship 7*) to the personal (the tiny harmonica and string of bells used by Gemini 6 astronauts Walter Schirra and Thomas Stafford to serenade Earth with their rendition of "Jingle Bells"). *Apollo to the Moon* also contains some of the Museum's great treasures: spacesuits worn by some of the first humans to walk upon another world.

The **F-1 rocket engine** near the gallery entrance hints at the enormous size of the rocket needed to send Apollo spacecraft to the Moon. The F-1 was the largest liquid-fuel rocket engine ever built in the United States, and the Saturn V the largest rocket in the world. Through the clever use of mirrors, one full engine and a one-quarter cutaway produce a view of the five-engine cluster at the base of the Saturn V's first stage. A detailed scale model of the 30-story-tall Saturn V and its launch tower stands nearby. Behind the F-1 display rests a single one-ton "shoe" from the crawler transporter vehicle used to carry the rocket and its tower to the launch area.

A full-size mock-up of a lunar module cockpit conveys the drama of a Moon landing. Visible through the two small triangular windows is film footage of the approaching lunar surface taken from the Apollo 17 lunar module. The shadow of the spacecraft appears on the surface just before touchdown, and you can hear the excitement in the voices of astronauts Eugene Cernan and Harrison Schmitt as they land on the Moon.

The central area of the gallery displays dozens of artifacts large and small. On one side are Gemini and Apollo fuel cells, a generator for powering instrument packages on the Moon, and the main control console from an Apollo command module simulator. On the other side is a wall displaying astronaut equipment, including many items from the Mercury missions of Alan Shepard and John Glenn and from Apollo 11. You can examine checklists and flight plans, navigational aids, survival gear, health equipment, garments, tools for in-flight maintenance and for collecting lunar samples, even a spare wire-mesh wheel and fender from the Apollo 17 lunar rover.

Other displays feature photographic gear, items from John Glenn's 1962 flight in *Friendship 7*, and the capsules and couches used by America's first spacefarers, the monkeys Able and Baker, in 1959. You can also examine packages of space food and personal hygiene

Five huge F-1 rocket engines were needed to lift the 30-story-tall Saturn V Moon rocket off the launch pad. Through the use of mirrors, one full engine and a one-quarter cutaway produce a view of the five-engine cluster at the base of the rocket's first stage.

equipment from the Mercury missions through the Space Shuttle era. Glenn was the first person to dine in space—he sucked on a tube of applesauce. By comparison, the Space Shuttle is a four-star restaurant. Items from the early shuttle years include standard utensils, a package of M&M chocolate candy, and cans of Pepsi and Coke specially engineered for consumption in space.

Beyond this cornucopia of artifacts are two lunar dioramas. Within them are scientific equipment of the type placed on the Moon, a **lunar rover** like those that astronauts drove on the last three lunar missions, and **historic spacesuits** worn on the Moon.

Beyond the Apollo dioramas are the rescue net and hoist used to lift Apollo 8 astronauts James Lovell, Frank Borman, and William Anders aboard the recovery helicopter after they returned from their historic first flight around the Moon; the hatch from the Apollo 11 command module *Columbia;* and the **Apollo command module** that ferried the final Skylab astronaut crew to that U.S. space station and back in 1973–74. An exhibit on the geology of the lunar surface includes samples of some of the 800 pounds of lunar rocks and soil brought back from the Moon.

Apollo 17 astronauts Eugene Cernan and Harrison Schmitt used a lunar rover like this one to explore areas far from their landing site. To the left is the spacesuit worn by Cernan, the last man to leave the Moon.

Opposite: The gallery displays an assortment of space food from Project Mercury through the Space Shuttle era. These soft drink cans were specially engineered for use in space.

Small treasures and other attractions:

Look for the model of a futuristic wheel-shaped space station designed by Wernher von Braun in the 1950s, and for the famous white vest worn by NASA flight controller Eugene Kranz during the aborted Apollo 13 mission. The "Apollo Stacks" room honors the astronauts from every Mercury, Gemini, and Apollo mission, and it also has copies of the metal plaques left behind by the six crews that landed on the Moon.

Far Left: Neil Armstrong and Buzz Aldrin wore these spacesuits when they became the first humans to walk on the Moon. Spacesuits from the Apollo program have become fragile over time, so Museum staff periodically replace the suits on display with others worn by Apollo astronauts.

Left: Standing about 12 feet tall, this detailed scale model of the Saturn V rocket and its launch tower helps convey the mammoth size of the vehicle that sent men to the Moon.

121

Exploring *the* Moon

Few who are old enough to recall have forgotten where they were on July 20, 1969, when astronaut Neil Armstrong stepped down from a craft like the one displayed here and became the first human to set foot on another world. Between 1969 and 1972, five more lunar modules landed on the Moon.

Lunar Module 2 displayed here is the real thing, the second lunar lander built for the Apollo program. The unmanned orbital test flight of the first lunar module was so successful that a second unmanned flight was deemed unnecessary. This lander was used instead for ground testing. Built for use in the airless environment of space, the lunar module did not need to be streamlined, and while fragile-looking it was sturdy enough for use in the Moon's low gravity. Its patchwork of flat-black panels and shiny film helped control heating and cooling.

An extensive lunar exploration program using robotic scouts and explorers preceded the manned lunar missions. Three types of space probes that transmitted images of the Moon, inspected its surface, and searched for Apollo landing sites hang overhead, along with a more recent lunar explorer. All four were used for testing.

The **Ranger** spacecraft were the first U.S. probes to send back close-up views of the Moon. Rangers 7, 8, and 9 transmitted thousands of pictures as they sped toward their crash landings. Millions of television viewers witnessed Ranger 9's descent to Moon, as the pictures it relayed were broadcast live on TV.

Five **Surveyor** spacecraft landed on the Moon and used a robotic arm and sampling scoop to examine the lunar soil. They confirmed that the Moon's surface could support astronauts and lunar landers.

Five **Lunar Orbiter** spacecraft sent back images used to locate landing sites; the last two mapped nearly all remaining lunar terrain.

Clementine was built to test lightweight instruments and components for a new generation of spacecraft. It orbited the Moon for two months in 1994 and mapped its entire surface, including polar areas never before photographed.

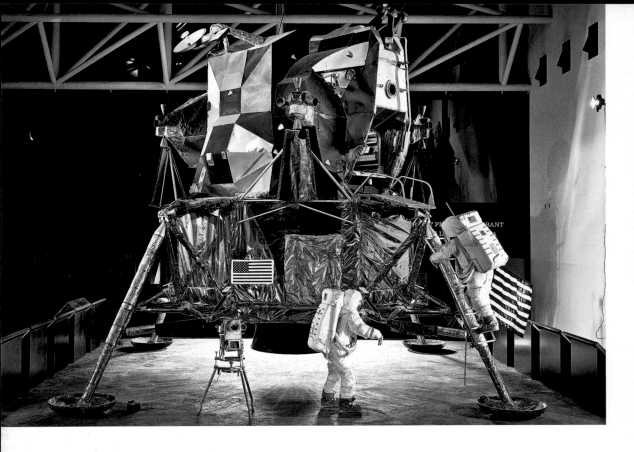

Above: Lunar Module 2 is one of two remaining lunar landers built for the Apollo missions.

Right: An astronaut descends the ladder of the lunar module in the *Exploring the Moon* gallery.

Opposite: An array of unmanned lunar exploration spacecraft hang above Lunar Module 2 in the *Exploring the Moon* gallery.

Overleaf: A video camera mounted in Lunar Module 2 enables you to look around inside. Note the pair of triangular windows.

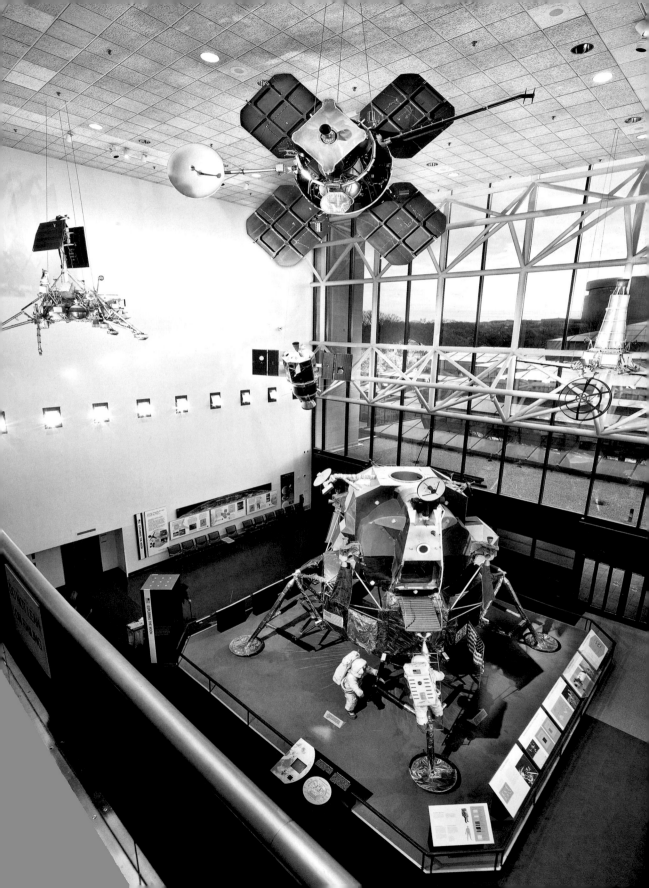

Looking *at* Earth

GALLERY 110

We are drawn to heights. As children we climb trees and hills, have an urge to get on top of things. Later we ascend mountains, not only for the challenge, but also for the sheer beauty of the vistas. We go to the top of the tallest building to look down upon our surroundings. We pay extra for the room with a view. The thrill of flight surely owes much to the incomparable bird's-eye view.

The view from above is practical too. We can identify friends and foes from a distance, spy on our enemies, guard our domain. We can monitor crops, spot fires, make better maps, report on the morning traffic. From even higher, we can watch weather systems form and approach. We can observe our world as a whole.

Looking at Earth explores the technology of aerial and space observation and its many uses. The gallery displays aircraft and spacecraft and examples of the photographic and imaging devices used on them. But most absorbing are the images themselves. Some are historic; others show scientific, military, or civil applications; others are simply beautiful. All allow us to examine the familiar from unfamiliar perspectives.

In 1860 a balloonist photographed Boston from above, marking the beginning of aerial photography in the United States. The following year near where the Museum now stands, Thaddeus Lowe ascended in a balloon to demonstrate its value as an observation platform. Lowe later used his balloon to observe Confederate troop movements—field glasses he used are on display. By the turn of the century, people were sending cameras aloft on kites, balloons, rockets, even birds. A miniature camera patented in 1903 was designed to be strapped to a pigeon and its shutter triggered by a timer. In 1925 a photographer took the first nighttime aerial photo by igniting a huge flash bomb in the sky above Rochester, New York, illuminating the city and startling its citizenry.

As the technology of flight evolved, dozens of applications for aerial photography developed. Images of coastlines, rivers, and rock

show how aerial photography has become an invaluable tool for geologists and geographers. Other images document the development of Washington, D.C. Some images, such as those showing the decades-old coal fires smoldering beneath Centralia, Pennsylvania, reveal how aerial photos can help assess environmental disasters.

Two airplanes hang in the gallery. The **de Havilland DH-4** was used during and after World War I for aerial observation and photography. This airplane carries two early Kodak cameras, and other aerial cameras displayed nearby trace the technology through World War II. Among the intriguing images on display here: the zigzagging trenches of the Western Front in World War I; the real "bridge on the River Kwai," built by prisoners of the Japanese in World War II; and efforts made to counteract aerial surveillance through camouflage.

The **Lockheed U-2** aircraft represents the Cold War use of aerial surveillance. Developed in the 1950s, the U-2 was designed to photograph the Soviet Union from altitudes too high for it to be intercepted. The Soviets managed to shoot down a U-2 in 1960 and captured its pilot, Francis Gary Powers. On display are the diary and secret journal Powers kept while in captivity, the rug he embroidered and in which he hid those documents when he was released, and a

Introduced as a bomber during World War I, the de Havilland DH-4 was also used for wartime observation and photoreconnaissance. DH-4s were also adapted for peacetime uses, such as forest patrols, geological surveys, photography, and mapping.

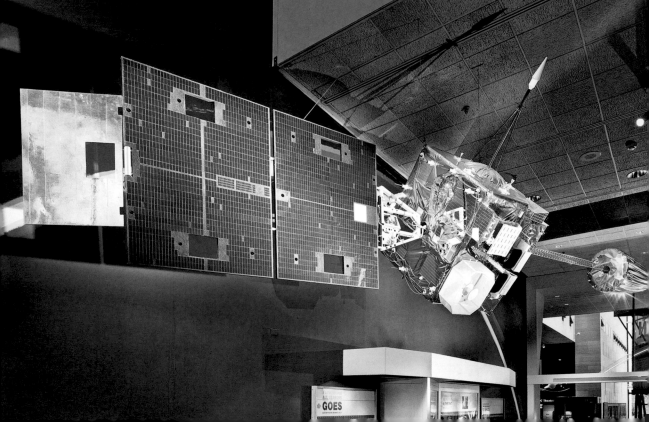

telegram from Soviet Premier Nikita Khrushchev to Powers's father regarding the fate of the captive pilot.

U-2s continued to play a vital surveillance role, especially in the Cuban Missile Crisis of 1962, depicted here in photographs and film. On display is a Hycon Model B panoramic camera, the type used to take the pictures that proved the existence of Soviet missiles in Cuba. By the 1960s, satellite spies in space were supplementing aerial reconnaissance. The Discoverer-13 reentry capsule on exhibit was the first object recovered from Earth orbit. It was used to test a system of satellites—code-named Corona and kept secret until the 1990s—that took photos of the Soviet Union from space and returned them to Earth for recovery and processing.

Space is the ultimate vantage point for looking at Earth. From there, cameras can take richly detailed images of geographic features, track weather systems, and monitor environmental changes. Infrared images can highlight thermal differences. Radar can map surface textures regardless of cloud cover or light conditions. Digital images can be processed and color enhanced to emphasize different features or produce three-dimensional views.

Landsat satellites have been monitoring the Earth since 1972. On display is a scale model of Landsat 4 and two generations of Landsat imagers, along with images used in applications ranging from agriculture to archaeology. The most familiar application of satellite imaging is the daily weather report. The prototype TIROS II represents the series of satellites that began operating in 1960 and gave us our first views of weather systems from space. A test version of ITOS exemplifies a later-generation TIROS satellite that operated during the 1970s. A small-scale model of a TIROS-N satellite represents yet another newer version.

Blues and purples mark an ozone hole of record size over Antarctica in this image made from data collected in 2004 by NASA's Aura satellite.

Opposite Above: The Lockheed U-2 photoreconnaissance airplane provided critical military intelligence during the Cold War. U-2s monitored military installations in the Soviet Union and Cuba and nuclear testing in China. This one was the first U-2 to fly over the Soviet Union.

Opposite Below: GOES satellites provide images of weather systems across the globe. Placed in a high-altitude orbit, each satellite remains over one spot on Earth and monitors the weather continuously across a single broad region.

The gallery also displays a scale-model GOES satellite. Each GOES is placed in a high orbit that keeps it positioned over a single spot on the Earth, enabling it to monitor a region continuously. GOES satellites provide much of the weather imagery on which we rely daily—one more benefit of our fascination with looking homeward from on high.

Small treasures and other attractions:

The gallery features sweeping photomurals of Washington, D.C., New York City, and the region surrounding Chesapeake Bay. Frequently updated video monitors in "What's New?" highlight new developments in the science and technology of looking at Earth. "Windows on Earth," a high-definition video display, allows you to "fly" around the world and view the Earth from the altitude of the International Space Station, then zoom in for an amazingly detailed view.

This GOES satellite image captured Hurricane Katrina making landfall over southeast Louisiana and southern Mississippi on August 29, 2005.

Opposite: In 1960 TIROS I became the world's first successful imaging weather satellite. Nine more TIROS series spacecraft followed, and they revolutionized weather monitoring and prediction.

Exploring *the* Planets

Asingle large spacecraft dominates the center of *Exploring the Planets:* a full-scale replica of Voyager. Beginning in 1979, two Voyager spacecraft blazed a trail of discovery through the outer solar system, swooping past numerous planets and moons. Like other robotic spacefarers, the Voyagers served as extensions of our senses, as surrogate eyes and ears and hands. They took pictures, measured spectra, recorded magnetic fields. The data the Voyagers sent back—especially the dazzling, close-up images of planets and moons—transformed our perspective of our distant planetary neighbors. We now know them not just as glowing orbs in a telescope or gleaming gems in the night sky, but as worlds as real and unique as our own.

Just inside the gallery entrance is a collage of photographs, each depicting a planet or moon we have only in recent decades been able to see so closely and clearly. *Exploring the Planets* takes you on a tour of this remarkable realm, as seen and sensed by the detectors aboard our robotic explorers.

An introductory section presents some historical highlights from our long journey of discovery. "Tools of Exploration" shows the various means by which we study other worlds, including ground-based, airborne, and orbital telescopes. Sections devoted to each planet, asteroids, and comets form the core of the gallery. "Comparing the Planets" explores geological similarities and differences, and computer monitors in "What's New?" display frequently updated images and information from current missions of exploration.

We have visited only one other world in person: our Moon. Twelve astronauts during six Apollo missions walked upon the lunar terrain and collected rock and soil samples. Apollo 12 astronauts carried lunar samples back to Earth in the suitcase-like container displayed in the "Tools" section. They also had the rare opportunity to retrieve hardware from an earlier mission. You can examine the TV camera they removed from the Surveyor 3 lander, which had been on the Moon for two and a half years.

The Moon and the inner planets are all rocky and relatively small, but otherwise quite distinctive. Images taken by Mariner 10 and MESSENGER show that airless and cratered Mercury looks much like our Moon. Venus, on the other hand, is cloud covered and hellishly hot. Magma has welled up from below and formed volcanoes, blistered Venus's surface with lava domes, and carved lava channels. The Magellan spacecraft obtained the images of Venus displayed here by using radar to penetrate the clouds and map the surface. A computer-generated flyover, created from Magellan images, provides a close-up view of Venus's tortured terrain.

Mars in particular has long captured our imagination, and scientists have explored it intensively in recent decades. Since Mariner 4 first flew by Mars in 1965 and returned a few fuzzy images, we've sent more robotic explorers to Mars than any other world. Numerous orbiters, landers, and rovers have journeyed to the Red Planet, and many are still at work.

The gallery's section on Mars displays some of the results of this exploration: a wealth of images and data that reveal Mars as a world of change, similar in many ways to Earth, but also strikingly different. It is a place of familiar geological processes and features, but it has

The gallery displays myriad images, collected by many types of spacecraft, of the solar system's diverse collection of worlds.

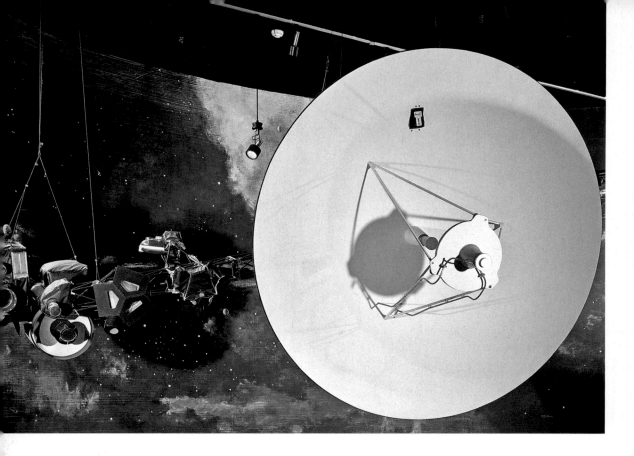

A replica of a Voyager spacecraft hangs in the center of the gallery. Beginning in 1979, two Voyager spacecraft visited the outer planets—Jupiter, Saturn, Uranus, and Neptune.

Opposite: A full-scale model of a Mars Exploration Rover, two of which landed on Mars in 2004. These twin "robot geologists" roved about the Martian terrain, searching for clues to the history of water on Mars.

produced canyons and volcanoes and dust storms of staggering size. Its landscape is a frozen and—as far as we know—lifeless desert, but one that bears overwhelming evidence that Mars was once a much wetter place and perhaps could have harbored life.

The centerpiece of the Mars section is a full-scale model of a **Mars Exploration Rover,** two of which—named Spirit and Opportunity—landed on Mars in 2004. These intrepid "robot geologists" journeyed far from their landing sites to search for answers about the history of water on Mars.

The four giant planets—Jupiter, Saturn, Uranus, and Neptune—are nothing like the worlds found closer to the Sun. Each is made mostly of gas and has no solid surface. Each embraces a large family of moons and is surrounded by thin rings. Yet every gas giant is different: Jupiter with its swirling cloud belts and its gigantic storm system known as the Great Red Spot; Saturn with its elegant rings; oddball Uranus, a world tipped on its side; and blue-green Neptune, with its frozen methane clouds and Great Dark Spot. Many of the moons of the outer planets are themselves strange wonders: sulfurous Io, whose active volcanoes continually reshape its surface; icy Europa, whose crust may conceal an ocean of water; cloud-shrouded Titan, with its

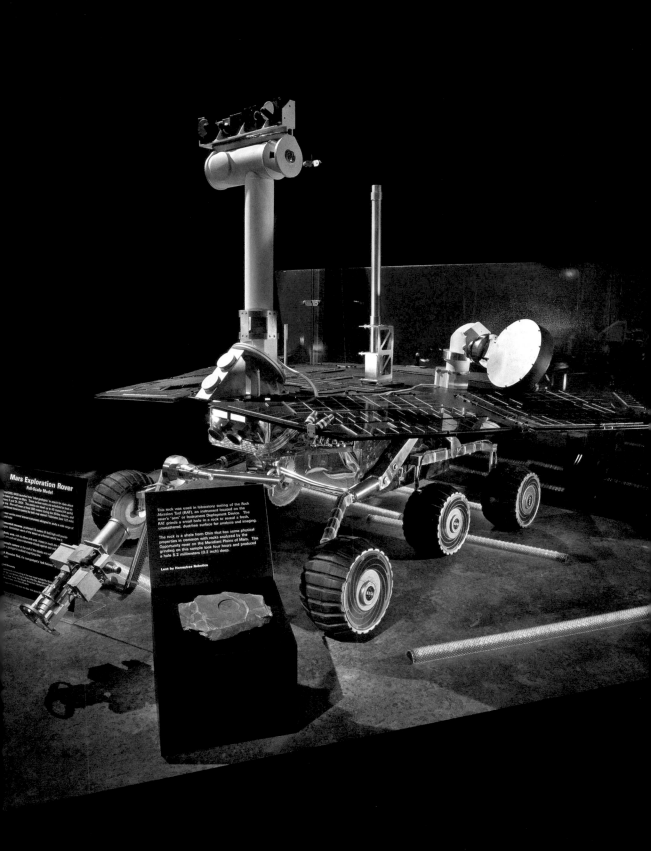

Mars Exploration Rover
Full-Scale Model

This rock was used in laboratory testing of the Rock Abrasion Tool (RAT), an instrument located on the rover's "arm" or Instruments Deployment Device. The RAT grinds a small hole in a rock to reveal a fresh, unweathered, dust-free surface for analysis and imaging.

The rock is a shale from Ohio that has some physical properties in common with rocks analyzed by the Opportunity rover on the Meridiani Plains of Mars. The grinding on this sample took four hours and produced a hole 5.2 millimeters (0.2 inch) deep.

Lent by Honeybee Robotics

liquid methane lakes; and super-frigid Triton, where nitrogen geysers erupt into the sky.

And then there is tiny icy Pluto, demoted in planetary status to dwarf planet in 2006. The New Horizons spacecraft is scheduled to visit this remote world for the first time in 2015.

Many of the images of the gas giants and their moons displayed here were taken by the Voyager spacecraft. Voyagers 1 and 2 visited Jupiter and Saturn from 1979 to 1981. Voyager 2 went on to visit Uranus in 1986 and Neptune in 1989. The **Voyager spacecraft** replica hanging overhead was made from components used in pre-launch

Visible in this Viking Orbiter view of Mars are the planet's north polar cap, the vast Valles Marineris canyon system (below center), and four huge volcanoes (at left).

engineering tests. While it may appear ungainly, Voyager is an engineering masterpiece. Its prominence here is fitting, for no other spacecraft has given us close-up views of so many planets and moons or had greater impact on our understanding of other worlds.

Small treasures and other attractions:

The introductory section displays a photographic plate used to discover Pluto and the handwritten message marking the discovery of Uranus's rings. In the Mars section, look for the global map of the Red Planet—complete with Martian canals—that astronomer Percival Lowell created in the early 1900s. You can test your knowledge about the planets by taking a computer quiz. In the "Exploring Comets" section, you can examine the circa-1910 Comet Seeker telescope and sketches of Comet Kohoutek drawn by Skylab astronauts in space.

The Mars Exploration Rover Spirit took this postcard-perfect view from the top of Husband Hill of the dunes and rocks of the Martian "Tennessee Valley."

Explore *the* Universe

The universe beyond our solar system is a realm beyond reach, the distances too vast to bridge with today's technology. We have walked on the Moon, scratched the surface of Mars, and probed the outer planets, but we can barely hope to reach even the nearest star. Luckily, the universe reveals itself to us in another way—through the light that pours down on us from the farthest depths of space and from almost as long ago as the beginning of time.

Deciphering what that light can tell us is an age-old obsession. Consider two artifacts displayed here: an Islamic astrolabe from 10 centuries ago and an imaging chip from the Hubble Space Telescope. One is a handheld astronomical calculator, the other a tiny silicon wafer that can capture photons of light from distant galaxies. Both were created to help answer the same basic question: What is the universe like?

The answer to that question has changed, sometimes suddenly and dramatically, as our tools for studying the universe have changed. *Explore the Universe* shows how our ideas about the universe evolved as we developed new tools to study it. The gallery presents the universe as discerned by the naked eye, and then shows how the telescope, photography, and spectroscopy revolutionized our understanding. The heart of the exhibition focuses on the universe today and reveals what astronomers now think about its structure and evolution.

For most of human history, our view of the universe was limited to what we could see in the sky: the Sun, Moon, and stars and a few perplexing points of light called planets. Studying the motions of these objects occupied astronomers for centuries. On exhibit are astrolabes, quadrants, an armillary sphere, and a celestial globe—all measuring tools, calculators, or maps of the heavens.

The ancient model of an Earth-centered universe began to give way to a Sun-centered universe after Galileo introduced the telescope to astronomy in the early 1600s. His telescope revealed multitudes of stars where none had ever been seen. This new universe had its own

mysteries. How far did it extend? What was its shape? What were those smudges of light that were neither stars nor planets?

A century and a half after Galileo, William Herschel searched for the answers and laid the foundation for our modern view of the universe. **Herschel's 20-foot telescope**, one of the great treasures in the gallery, was his favorite among the many large telescopes he built. He used this famous instrument in the late 1700s and early 1800s to create a crude map of the Milky Way and to catalog those smudges of light, the nebulae.

To record what he observed, Herschel had to draw what he saw through his telescope. The introduction of photography enabled astronomers to create far more precise and detailed images. Many great observatories soon arose. Greatest among them in the early 1900s was the Mount Wilson Observatory near Los Angeles, represented here by a scaled-down observatory dome. Within the dome is the **observing cage from the 100-inch Hooker Telescope**, which astronomer Edwin Hubble used to make two momentous discoveries: that galaxies fill the universe and that the universe is expanding.

This latter discovery was made possible by spectroscopy— spreading light from a star or galaxy into a rainbow of colors called a

Discoverer of the planet Uranus in 1781, William Herschel built some of the largest, most powerful telescopes in the world. His favorite and most famous was his 20-foot telescope. The telescope's wooden tube, mounted on a scaled-down replica of its framework, is on display here.

Early astronomers used many kinds of instruments for measuring or calculating the positions of objects in the sky. Shown here are a celestial globe (top), a quadrant (bottom), and two astrolabes.

Opposite: Using Mount Wilson Observatory's 100-inch Hooker Telescope, Edwin Hubble transformed our understanding of the size and structure of the universe. This diorama features the telescope's original observing cage and camera.

spectrum. Unique as a fingerprint, an object's spectrum can reveal chemical composition and relative motion. You can examine spectroscopic equipment from the 1800s to the late 1900s, including the prime focus spectrograph from the 200-inch Hale Telescope at the Palomar Observatory in Southern California.

Space-age technology and the digital revolution have transformed how we explore the universe. Digital light detectors and processors have enhanced the power of telescopes. The CCD (charge-coupled device), an electronic chip used to record light, has largely replaced photography. Our view of the universe now encompasses not only visible light, but also radio, infrared, ultraviolet, x-rays, and gamma rays. Each requires specialized detectors.

Models of orbital observatories—the Cosmic Background Explorer (COBE), Hubble Space Telescope, and Chandra X-ray Observatory—hang overhead. Other space hardware includes the optically flawless **backup mirror for the Hubble Space Telescope** and optical elements from the Hubble's original Wide-Field/Planetary Camera. Nearby is the **Faint Object Spectrograph.** This phone-booth–size device, retrieved from the Hubble, provided the first conclusive evidence of a black hole. Also here are instruments used by COBE to detect the cosmic

background radiation or "fading flash" from the big bang, the event that astronomers think set the expansion of the universe in motion, and a full-scale reconstruction of the **WMAP** satellite, which mapped the cosmic background radiation with greater sensitivity and resolution than ever before. You can also examine the **Hopkins Ultraviolet Telescope**, carried aboard the Space Shuttle and used to measure the matter between the galaxies.

With innovations in digital imaging, a new generation of ground-based telescopes—exemplified by models of the Keck and Gemini observatories—along with optically upgraded older telescopes, can now compete with space-based telescopes in image clarity and resolution. Balloon-borne instruments, such as Boomerang, also remain vital tools.

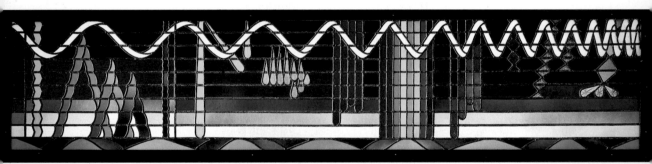

This stained-glass panel depicts the full range of light that shines onto the Earth from space. The light rays are arranged by wavelength, from longest (radio waves) to shortest (gamma rays). Also depicted are meteors, an aurora, and high-energy particles called cosmic rays.

Opposite: This backup mirror for the Hubble Space Telescope was never given its reflective coating of aluminum, so you can see its lightweight internal structure. Unlike the mirror on the Hubble, this one is optically flawless.

Astronomers today are focusing on the structure, evolution, and fate of the universe, and such mysteries as dark matter—unseen material that may account for most of the universe's mass. Questions people have pondered for millennia—What is the universe? How old is it? How big? How did it begin?—remain open for astronomers of today and tomorrow.

Small treasures and other attractions:

One of the strangest devices here is a detector resembling a TV tube, 11,200 of which line the gigantic subterranean water tank that is the Super-Kamiokande neutrino observatory. Less exotic but also intriguing are a pigeon trap that played a role in the Nobel Prize–winning discovery of the cosmic background radiation, and an image of the electromagnetic spectrum rendered in stained glass. Interactive exhibits invite you to delve into hot topics in current astronomy, learn what's new at many observatories, and track the current positions of such orbiting telescopes as Hubble, COBE, and Chandra.

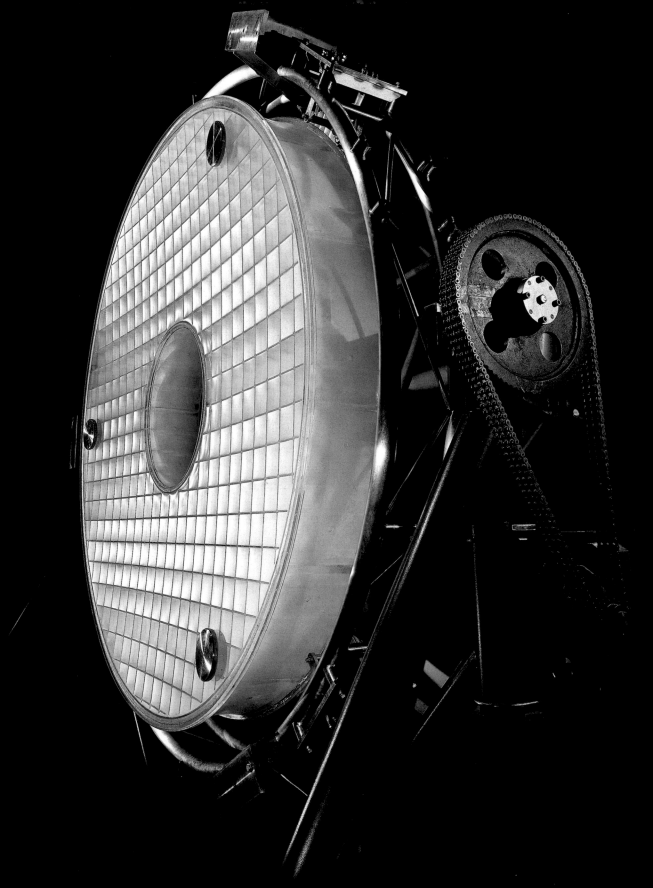

OTHER THINGS

You can walk through a section of a Boeing 757 airliner fuselage with its internal sttructure exposed in the *How Things Fly* gallery.

TO DO

How Things Fly

Although air travel has become commonplace and even spaceflight now seems almost routine, flight has never lost its magic or mystery. The magic derives from being able to see the world from the perspective of a bird or to view a planet or moon from space. The mystery lies in the means: How *does* an airplane stay aloft? How can something as insubstantial as air support all that weight? Why do you become "weightless" in space? Once you get there, how can you propel yourself with no air to push against?

These and many other questions are answered in *How Things Fly,* a gallery devoted to explaining the basic principles that allow aircraft and spacecraft to fly. The emphasis here is "hands-on." Dozens of exhibits invite you to push, pull, press, lift, slide, handle, touch, twist, turn, spin, bend, and balance. Here you can discover for yourself answers to things you've always wondered about flight.

The entrance area introduces the four forces of flight—lift, drag, thrust, weight—and two key aspects of the flight environment: gravity and air. You can test your strength against air pressure and learn how buoyancy makes a hot-air balloon float in midair. You can get a real feel for air pressure at different altitudes by lifting metal bars that correspond to air pressure at sea level, Denver, and the top of Mount Everest. Other exhibits explain the effect of gravity and show how much you would weigh on other worlds.

The section called "Winging It" demystifies how a wing works. The basic principles are simple: as air speeds up, its pressure goes down; and differences in pressure can push things around. Wings are shaped to create an imbalance in air pressure that produces an upward force. A wind tunnel and other devices use blowing air or flowing liquid to demonstrate this effect. Drag, or air resistance, depends on how streamlined an object is and how fast it is moving. You can experiment with different shapes to see which create less drag, and use a computer program to compare the lift and drag created by four kinds of airplane wings.

Flying at supersonic speeds alters the dynamics of how wings work. Exhibits in the "Faster Than Sound" section demonstrate how lift and drag affect an aircraft flying at very high speeds. The most remarkable exhibit here is a supersonic wind tunnel. It enables you to view the shadow of an actual shock wave, which is created by a blast of air moving at supersonic speed past a small object. Other exhibits show how the shape of an airplane can reduce the effects of shock waves and supersonic drag.

Exhibits on "Getting Aloft" illuminate the crucial role of thrust. Actual cutaway engines help show how piston, turbojet, and rocket engines work. A touchable, sectioned propeller demonstrates that the blade is really "a wing with a twist." By lifting a model of a Saturn V Moon rocket, you can compare the weight of its payload with the weight of the rocket and fuel required to lift the payload into space.

Lift and drag are irrelevant in space, where an environment of "Gravity and No Air" defines how things fly. Exhibits in this section reveal that an object in orbital flight is really falling, and that falling— not lack of gravity—causes the sensation of weightlessness. Newton's and Kepler's laws of motion rule the cosmic road. An air track and computer programs on gravity and orbits show how these laws apply to spaceflight.

Above: You can climb into the cockpit of a real Cessna 150 and manipulate the controls.

Below: Adopted by an elementary school in Pine, Colorado, in 1993 to stimulate student interest in geography, science, and exploration, Magellan T. Bear has traveled around the world, under the sea, and even into space.

Flight also involves stability and control. In the section on "Staying Aloft," you can climb into the cockpit of a **Cessna 150,** a small airplane in which many pilots learn to fly, and manipulate some of the controls. You can try controlling a model Cessna suspended in stream of air, and see how the ailerons, elevator, and rudder affect its orientation. Controlling a spacecraft is trickier, requiring the use of thrusters or spinning wheels to alter its attitude. You can try changing your own attitude while sitting on a rotatable chair and spinning a handheld wheel, or balance a rod on your fingertip to learn about stability, or test your reaction time against that of a champion aerobatic pilot.

The final section provides a look at "Structures and Materials." You enter this area through a section of a Boeing 757 airliner fuselage with its internal structure exposed. Mounted on the wall is part of another Cessna 150, this one with its skin removed to show its underlying structure. Touchable materials illustrate some of the issues that affect how aircraft and spacecraft are built: reducing weight while maintaining strength, the pros and cons of using various materials, the effect of stress on structures, and protecting craft and crew from the frictional heat of hypersonic *(much* faster than sound) flight.

Exhibit labels throughout the gallery relate aspects of flight to other phenomena, answer nagging questions (How can an airplane fly upside down?), and suggest demonstrations illustrating the forces of flight that you can try yourself. The gallery also has an amphitheater, where live presentations take place.

Small treasures and other attractions:

Youngsters might like to visit to Magellan T. Bear, a well-traveled stuffed animal who has flown around the world, sailed under the sea in a submarine, flown with the Blue Angels, and even ridden aboard the Space Shuttle. Magellan sits on one of the seats in the Boeing 757 airliner section, awaiting a new adventure.

A corps of student explainers are on hand in *How Things Fly* to answer questions, provide assistance, and give demonstrations.

Flight *and the* Arts

Tucked away in a corner on the second floor, *Flight and the Arts* is overlooked by many visitors. On one hand this is unfortunate, for they have missed many wonderful exhibitions of art, photography, and popular culture relating to aviation and space. On the other hand, those who do visit the gallery usually find it a welcome refuge of quiet and calm in an otherwise bustling museum. The gallery features traveling exhibitions produced by the Smithsonian and other institutions, special temporary shows created exclusively for the Museum, and displays of the National Air and Space Museum's own substantial collection of aviation and space art.

Above and Left: "Generous Friends: Building an Art Collection for the National Air and Space Museum" showcased some of the more than 4,000 objects in the Museum's art collection.

Opposite: *Aerial Inspirations* featured the works of South Carolina artist, photographer, and pilot Mary Edna Fraser. Her dyed silk batiks depicted scenes inspired by aerial photographs and satellite imagery.

Following Pages Above: The Lockheed Martin IMAX Theater presents a variety of 70 mm, large-format films on a huge screen that measures about 50 feet tall by 75 feet wide.

Following Pages Below: A video projection system and special effects projectors create full-dome scenes and such phenomena as aurora displays.

Planetarium,
IMAX THEATER, & FLIGHT SIMULATORS

Under the indoor sky of the Albert Einstein Planetarium, you can gaze up at an impressive simulation of the night sky projected on a dome 70 feet across. At the heart of this chamber is the Zeiss Model VIa planetarium projector. An engineering marvel and an extraordinary teaching tool, the Zeiss accurately reproduces the positions and motions of the stars, Sun, Moon, and planets and can show how the sky appears on any night of any year from anywhere on Earth. A full-dome video projection system and special effects projectors turn the theater into an immersive multimedia experience. The planetarium offers multimedia shows on astronomy and space, as well as live presentations that do what only a planetarium can— show you what's visible overhead that night and demonstrate how to find your way around the sky using constellations and bright stars.

To get a sense of what it's like to fly without leaving the ground, or to experience views of our world from the magnificent vantage of space, visit the Lockheed Martin IMAX Theater. Large-format, 70 mm films are presented here several times a day, projected on a huge screen that fills your field of view, and enhanced by a state-of-the-art digital sound system. The effect can be truly transporting; you may find yourself gripping the armrests of your seat. You can choose from several films on topics relating to aviation and space, including *To Fly!*, the Museum's longest running film and still a favorite.

In the Museum's *Flight Simulators* gallery, you can climb aboard interactive flight simulators that you and a co-pilot can "fly." Or you can ride larger simulators that seat up to eight people and provide a variety of flight experiences, including flying vintage or modern airplanes, piloting the Space Shuttle, or taking a cosmic voyage.

STEVEN F. UDVAR

Towering over the entrance to the
Udvar-Hazy Center is the Donald D.
Engen Observation Tower, named
in honor of the late director of the
National Air and Space Museum.

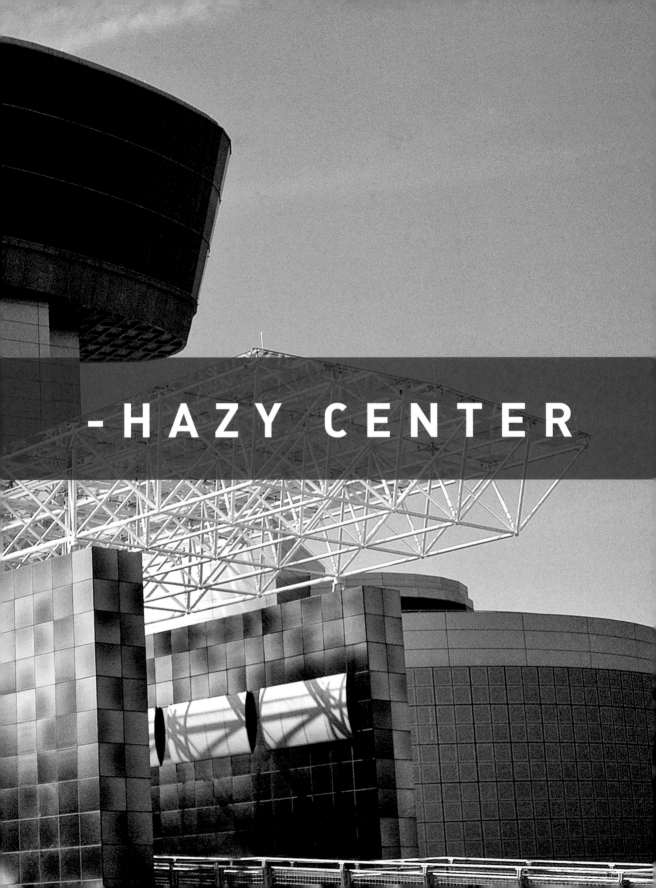

- HAZY CENTER

Steven F. Udvar-Hazy Center

On December 15, 2003, two days before the 100th anniversary of the Wright brothers' historic flights at Kitty Hawk, a companion facility to the National Air and Space Museum opened on the grounds of Washington Dulles International Airport in Northern Virginia. Named for the man whose $60-million pledge helped launch the project (at the time the largest-ever donation by an individual to the Smithsonian), the Steven F. Udvar-Hazy Center is a stunning new addition to the world's most popular museum.

The Center is enormous in size—the Boeing Aviation Hangar alone is about three football fields long and ten stories tall, large enough to contain the entire National Air and Space Museum building on the National Mall. The James S. McDonnell Space Hangar, the other exhibition hall, is spacious enough to house the prototype Space Shuttle orbiter *Enterprise,* with plenty of room to spare for rockets, missiles, satellites, spacecraft, and more. Unlike the Museum's old Garber Facility, the Udvar-Hazy Center provides a state-of-the-art, climate-controlled environment for the artifacts and allows for better viewing. And like the museum on the Mall, you can visit the Center every day of the year but Christmas.

There you will find more than 150 aircraft and about as many large space artifacts, along with thousands of smaller objects—no one has tried to count them all. Many have never before been on exhibit.

Artifacts are grouped into thematic areas, each anchored by an "exhibit station" that provides historical context. Display cases throughout the hangars display smaller artifacts. The Udvar-Hazy Center also features the Donald D. Engen Observation Tower, which provides an excellent view of aircraft coming in for landings at the nearby airport runways; the Airbus IMAX Theater; and the Claude Moore Education Center, for use by visiting teachers and students. Still to come: an addition that will house the Mary Baker Engen Restoration Hangar, with its mezzanine viewing area where you can

NASA built this human-size android for testing spacesuits in the 1960s.

Opposite: The Center showcases an extraordinary collection of World War II aircraft. Here, a Republic P-47D Thunderbolt rests in front of the Boeing B-29 Superfortress *Enola Gay*, the airplane that dropped the atomic bomb on Hiroshima.

Overleaf Above: The Steven F. Udvar-Hazy Center lies a few miles south of Dulles Airport's passenger terminals. The long Boeing Aviation Hangar is large enough to contain the entire National Air and Space Museum's National Mall building. The James S. McDonnell Space Hangar juts out from the back side.

Overleaf Below: The Lockheed SR-71 Blackbird, a reconnaissance plane, is the world's fastest jet-propelled aircraft. On its final flight before being turned over to the Museum, this one set a speed record by flying from Los Angeles to Washington, D.C., in just over one hour.

watch preservation and restoration projects in progress; an archive area; collections processing and storage facilities; and the Emil Buehler Conservation Laboratory.

Boeing Aviation Hangar

The Boeing Aviation Hangar contains three levels of hanging aircraft above dozens more resting on the floor. They include many of the largest in the Museum's collection: the only surviving Boeing 307 Stratoliner, the first pressurized airliner; the Boeing 367-80, the prototype for the famous Boeing 707 airliner; the Boeing B-29 Superfortress Enola Gay, the airplane that dropped the atomic bomb on Hiroshima; a Lockheed Super Constellation airliner flown by Air Force and Air National Guard units; a Lockheed SR-71 Blackbird, the world's fastest jet aircraft; and an Air France Concorde, the first supersonic jetliner. Among or above these are scores of smaller aircraft both famous and obscure, one-of-a-kinds and last-of-a-kinds, vintage airplanes returned to pristine condition, and some yet to be fully restored. They cover nearly the entire range of aviation: pre-1920 aircraft; commercial, general, business, and sport aviation; vertical flight; and military aircraft from World War I and World War II, Korea and Vietnam, the Cold War era, and beyond. Engine buffs will enjoy strolling along "engine row," a veritable walk of fame of aircraft propulsion technology.

Exhibit stations in the Aviation Hangar cover pre-1920 aviation, military aviation from the 1920s through the modern era, vertical flight, commercial aviation, business aviation, sport aviation, ultralight aircraft, and aerobatic flight.

James S. McDonnell Space Hangar

Clustered around the *Enterprise* in the James S. McDonnell Space Hangar are rockets and missiles; spacecraft and other artifacts relating to human spaceflight; satellites used for commercial, military, and

The Aviation Hangar houses well over 100 aircraft hung at three levels and parked on the floor. In the foreground is a Vought F4U-1D Corsair, with its distinctive inverted gull-wing design.

Opposite Above: Parked near a row of World War II Japanese aircraft are the yellow Northrop N-1M flying wing and the Northrop P-61C Black Widow with its distinctive twin tail booms.

Opposite Below: Surrounded by exhibit cases, rockets, missiles, satellites, and other artifacts, the Space Shuttle *Enterprise* is the centerpiece of the Space Hangar.

scientific applications; and objects used for space science research. To name just a few: a Redstone missile, a vehicle used to launch the first U.S. satellites and astronauts into space; a Ritchey grinding machine from 1890s, used to craft large telescope mirrors; a human-size NASA-built android used for spacesuit testing in the 1960s; the Mobile Quarantine Facility that housed the Apollo 11 astronauts upon their return from the Moon; a Pegasus XL, an air-launched vehicle for boosting satellites into orbit; and the mother ship model from the 1977 film *Close Encounters of the Third Kind*.

Exhibit stations in the Space Hangar cover applications satellites, human spaceflight, rockets and missiles, and space science.

The world's first supersonic airliner, the Concorde was a joint venture of Air France and British Airways. Concordes went out of service in 2003 while the Udvar-Hazy Center was being built. Planned aircraft locations were quickly reshuffled to accommodate this newly donated Air France Concorde.

The Paul E. Garber

PRESERVATION, RESTORATION, & STORAGE FACILITY

In Silver Hill, Maryland, a few miles from the National Mall, is a compound of more than 30 windowless metal buildings enclosed by a tall chain-link fence. The only thing about the place that might catch your eye is the Polaris missile standing in the parking lot. But this complex once housed the most amazing collection of aeronautical artifacts outside of the National Air and Space Museum itself.

The facility was created in the mid-1950s to store the large collection of aircraft and artifacts given to the Museum by the

U.S. Army Air Forces after World War II. It became the Museum's preservation, restoration, and storage facility and opened to the public for tours in 1977 as the "no-frills" Silver Hill Museum. In 1980 it was renamed for Paul E. Garber, the National Air Museum's first curator and the driving force behind the facility's creation.

The Garber Facility accommodated more than 200 aircraft, as well as engines, rockets, spacecraft, models, weapons, uniforms, memorabilia, and other hardware. But it never adequately served the Museum's storage and preservation needs. The buildings were crammed with aircraft, most fully assembled, some still in pieces, all snugly arranged among countless other objects to make the

most of the precious space. Most of the buildings lack humidity and temperature controls, essential to the long-term survival of the artifacts.

In 2003 the staff began moving the artifacts to the Museum's new Steven F. Udvar-Hazy Center, a process that continues today. The facility still contains the Museum's artifact restoration shop, part of the Museum Archives (both of which will move to the Udvar-Hazy Center), and exhibit production shops. Although still in use, the Garber Facility is no longer open for tours.

The Garber Facility houses part of the Museum Archives, which preserves a wide range of photo and document collections.

Opposite: Skilled craftspeople conserve and restore aircraft and other museum artifacts at the Garber Facility. This work will move to the Steven F. Udvar-Hazy Center when a new restoration facility is completed there.

General Information

LOCATIONS: The **National Air and Space Museum** is on the National Mall at Independence Avenue and 6th Street SW. Entrances are on Independence Avenue and Jefferson Drive. The **Steven F. Udvar-Hazy Center** is near Washington Dulles International Airport at 14390 Air and Space Museum Parkway, Chantilly, Virginia. The entrance is off Route 28.

ADMISSION: Free to all visitors.

HOURS: Open daily (except December 25) from 10:00 a.m. to 5:30 p.m. Extended spring/summer hours are determined annually.

INFORMATION SERVICES: Welcome Centers staffed by Visitor Services volunteers are located near the entrances to both museums. For Smithsonian information call 202-633-1000 (voice), 202-357-1729 (TTY), or 202-357-2020 (Spanish). Send queries by e-mail to info@si.edu, or visit the Smithsonian website at www.si.edu.

TOURS: Highlight tours are given by Museum docents daily at 10:30 a.m. and 1:00 p.m. at both museums. Audio tours are not available. The Paul E. Garber Facility is no longer open for tours.

GROUPS: Groups of adults (20 persons minimum) wanting tours or movie or planetarium tickets must make reservations at least two weeks (and no more than six months) in advance. Tours for people with sight or hearing impairments may be arranged with at least two weeks notice (no minimum number required). School group reservations for tours, programs, and science demonstrations must be made in writing at least three weeks in advance (no minimum number required); request a copy of the Museum's *School Programs Guide*. For reservations and information, use the online form at www/nasm.si.edu /tickets, call Monday through Friday 202-633-2563 (voice) or 202-357-1505 (TTY), fax 202-633-1957, e-mail nasmtours@si.edu, or, for school groups, visit www.nasm.si.edu/education/.

PUBLIC TRANSPORTATION: The closest Metro (subway) stop to the National Air and Space Museum is the L'Enfant Plaza station on the Yellow/Green and Blue/Orange lines. For more information call Metrorail at 202-637-7000 (voice) or 202-638-3780 (TTY) or visit www.wmata.com. There is no direct public transportation between Washington, D.C., and the Udvar-Hazy Center. However, the Center can be reached by a low-cost shuttle bus from the main terminal at Washington Dulles International Airport.

PARKING: The National Air and Space Museum does not have public parking, but there are many commercial parking lots in the area. Limited on-street parking is available, including handicapped spaces. Pay parking is available at the Udvar-Hazy Center. You can also purchase an annual parking pass; phone 703-572-4102 or e-mail uhcparkingpass@si.edu.

PHOTOGRAPHY: Handheld and personal video cameras are permitted. Monopods are also allowed, but the use of tripods is prohibited.

PETS: Only certified assistance animals are permitted in the Museum.

WHERE TO EAT: The Wright Place Food Court is on the first·floor, east end of the National Air and Space Museum. A McDonald's and McCafé are on the entrance level of the Udvar-Hazy Center.

SHOPPING: The Museum Store at the National Air and Space Museum is on the first floor near the entrance. The Udvar-Hazy Center's Museum Store is on the entrance level. Other smaller shops and kiosks are located in both museums.

THEATERS: Large-format films are presented on giant screens in IMAX theaters at both museums. Simulations of the night sky and programs on astronomy and space are presented in the Einstein Planetarium at the National Air and Space Museum. For show schedules and information or to purchase tickets, visit www.nasm.si.edu/imax or call 202-633-4629.

ACCESSIBILITY INFORMATION: Both locations offer access ramps and elevators. All theaters are wheelchair accessible, and most shows offer audio descriptions and/or closed captioning. Wheelchairs are available at both locations free of charge; inquire at the Welcome Center or Security Desk. Limited materials in Braille are available at the Welcome Center. Tours for persons who have visual, hearing, or other impairments may be arranged at least two weeks in advance by calling 202-633-2563.

MUSEUM WEBSITE: For more information on the National Air and Space Museum and Steven F. Udvar-Hazy Center, visit www.nasm.si.edu.

Along with aviation- and space-related books and products for sale, the three-level Museum Store displays a few artifacts from the Museum's collections, including a Pitts Special aerobatic airplane.

Photography Credits

Legend: **B** = bottom, **C** = center, **L** = left, **R** = right, **T** = top
CEPS Center for Earth and Planetary Studies (at NASM)
JPL Jet Propulsion Laboratory
NASM National Air and Space Museum
NASA National Aeronautics and Space Administration
SI Smithsonian Institution
USGS U.S. Geological Survey

Where available, Smithsonian photo numbers are listed in parentheses.

i, Eric Long; iv–v, Dane Penland; vi T, Eric Long (XV4A0095w); vi TC, Eric Long (2008-10049); vi BC, Eric Long (2008-369); vi B, Eric Long (2008-369); vii T, Eric Long (2005-15152); vii C, Eric Long (98-15680); vii B, Dane Penland (WEB10979-2008h); viii, Mark Avino (90-6015); 1, Carolyn Russo (2000-1168-1A); 2, Eric Long (XV4A0100.a); 3, Eric Long (XV4A0124-2); 4, SI photo (76-13966-12A); 6, Carolyn Russo; 7, SI photo (A-30599); 9, SI photo (A-48826-A); 10, SI photo (73-4622); 13, Eric Long (XV4A0031); 14, Eric Long (2005-3506); 17, Mark Avino (92-2946); 19, Eric Long (2008-10049); 20, Eric Long; 21, Eric Long (97-16234); 22 T, Dane Penland (80-3070); 22–23, Eric Long (2007-12576-2); 24, Eric Long (2000-8959-6); 25, Eric Long (2009-4950); 26, Carolyn Russo; 27 T, Eric Long (2005-176); 27 B, Eric Long (2005-30510); 28, Eric Long (2008-10057); 28–29, Eric Long (2006-4543); 30-31, Eric Long (2008-339); 33, Eric Long (2009-5176); 34, Eric Long (2008-354); 35, Eric Long (2009-5175); 36–37, Eric Long (2007-16000-2); 38, Eric Long (2008-3776); 39, Eric Long (2008-369); 40 T, Eric Long (NL9F4876); 40 B, Eric Long (2008-377); 41, Eric Long (2008-367); 43, Eric Long (2003-35575); 44–45, SI photo (2003-3463); 46, SI photo (2002-16615); 47, Eric Long (2006-28254); 48, Eric Long (97-16653); 48–49, Eric Long (2006-29558); 51, Eric Long (2005-15502); 52, Eric Long (98-15441); 53 T, Eric Long (2001-2640); 53 B, Eric Long (2005-20387); 54 T, Eric Long (2006-

29567); 54 B, Eric Long (2006-29569); 57, Eric Long (2005-22896); 58, Eric Long (2006-29564); 59 T, Eric Long (2006-26426); 59 B, Eric Long (2001-10347); 60, Eric Long (98-15919); 61, Eric Long (2009-4944); 63 T, Eric Long (2005-5390); 63 B, Eric Long (2005-3735); 64–65, Eric Long (97-17440); 66, Eric Long (97-15873); 67 T, Eric Long (2005-4700); 67 B, Eric Long (2005-5308); 69, Dane Penland (97-15335); 70 T, Eric Long (2006-25765); 70 B, Dane Penland; 71, Eric Long (2006-25766); 72 T, Eric Long (2005-22902); 72 B, Mark Avino (95-8900); 73 T, Eric Long (97-16073); 73 B, Eric Long (99-15624); 75 T, Eric Long (2005-14109); 75 B, Eric Long and Mark Avino (97-15363); 76–77, Eric Long (XV4A0071); 78, Dane Penland (80-2090); 79 T, Eric Long (97-15875); 79 B, Eric Long (XV4A0133); 80 B, Eric Long (97-15874); 80–81, Mark Avino (92-6535); 83, Eric Long (2005-15500); 84 T, Eric Long (2005-15501); 84 B, Eric Long (2005-15154); 85, Eric Long (XV4A7882-2); 86–87, Eric Long (2005-4698); 89, Eric Long (2001-2637); 90, Eric Long and Mark Avino; 91, SI photo; 92 B, Eric Long (2005-5712); 92–93, Mark Avino (2000-4632); 95, Eric Long (2007-29649); 96–97, Eric Long (2006-935); 98, Eric Long (2007-29637); 99, Eric Long (2006-1768); 101, Eric Long (2008-4232); 102 T, Eric Long (2008-2551); 102 B, Eric Long (2008-2552); 103, Eric Long (2008-2553); 104–105, Eric Long (2002-19565); 107, Eric Long (98-15989); 108, Eric Long (2005-15152); 109, Eric Long (2007-29755); 110,

Eric Long (2006-2099); 111, Eric Long (97-16254-3); 112, Mark Avino (96-16364); 113, Eric Long (97-16261-12); 114 T, Eric Long (XV4A0005-2); 114 B, Eric Long (97-15886-2); 115, Eric Long (2005-22900); 117, Eric Long (XV4A0019b); 118–119, Eric Long (99-15255); 119 B, Eric Long (99-15176); 120–121, Eric Long (99-15254); 121, Eric Long (99-15144); 123, Eric Long (99-15227); 124 T, Mark Avino (99-15231); 124 B, Eric Long (2006-17354); 125, Eric Long (2009-5256); 127, Eric Long (2006-25885); 128 T, Eric Long (2001-2243); 128 B, Eric Long (2006-25899); 129, NASA; 130, NASA; 131, Carolyn Russo (95-840); 133, NASA/CEPS; 134, Eric Long (99-15412); 135, Eric Long (2005-2062-4); 136, NASA/JPL/USGS; 137, NASA/JPL/Cornell; 139, Eric Long (2001-10222); 140, Eric Long (2001-5337); 141, Eric Long (2001-9895); 142, Eric Long (2001-7443); 143, Eric Long (2001-6718); 144–145, Eric Long; 147 T, Eric Long (2007-10732); 147 B, Eric Long (98-15573-5); 149, Eric Long (2007-12556); 150, Carolyn Russo (94-13184); 151 T,Eric Long; 151 B, Eric Long; 153 T, Eric Long (2009-4947); 153B, Eric Long (98-15680); 154–155, Dane Penland (2004-56492); 157 T, Eric Long (2004-31749-9); 157 B, Dane Penland (2006-2744); 158, Eric Long (2004-56232); 159, Dane Penland (2006-2327); 160, Dane Penland (2005-413); 161 T, Dane Penland (WEB 10979-2008h); 161 B, Dane Penland; 162–163, Eric Long (WEB 10596-2006h); 164, Eric Long (2008-1739); 165, Eric Long (2001-1386-A); 167, Eric Long (2000-9549)

SECOND FLOOR

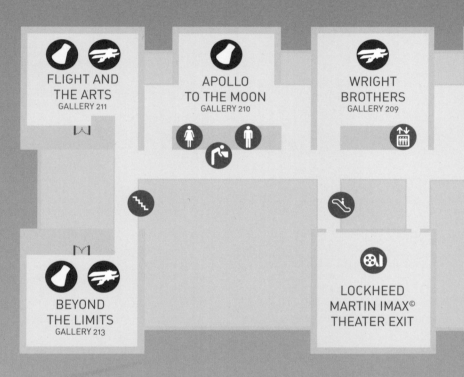

FLIGHT AND THE ARTS
GALLERY 211

APOLLO TO THE MOON
GALLERY 210

WRIGHT BROTHERS
GALLERY 209

BARON HILTON PIONEERS OF FLIGHT
GALLERY 208

BEYOND THE LIMITS
GALLERY 213

LOCKHEED MARTIN IMAX© THEATER EXIT

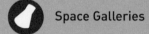 Space Galleries

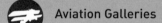 Baby Care Station

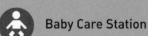 Food Service

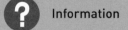 Aviation Galleries

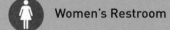 Men's Restroom

 Simulators

? Information

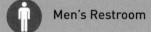 Women's Restroom

 Tickets

Museum Store

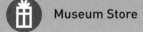 Family Restroom

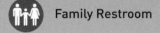 Theater

Emergency Exits

 Water Fountain

 Telephones

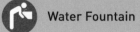